Principles for

Improving Your Life

inspired by the teachings of F M Alexander

ANTHONY JAMES TAYLOR

A Gil Books first edition, published in the United Kingdom by Groups In Learning (Gil).

A CIP catalogue record for this book is available from the British Library.

ISBN 0 9526320 2 0

Lay out and design: Ben Cole

All photographs copyright and by kind permission of Mark Simmons Photography, Bristol. (www.marksimmonsphotography.co.uk)
Except picture of F M Alexander, copyright and courtesy of The Society of Teachers of the Alexander Technique, London.
And pictures of John Gil, and author on back cover, courtesy and copyright: Gee, Bristol.

Printed and bound in Great Britain by MPG Books, Bodmin

Gil Books
10 Charlotte Street
Bristol
BS1 5PX
United Kingdom
+ 44 (0)117 9253413

Gil Books
Box No. 269
793 A Foothill Boulevard
San Luis Obispo
CA, 93405
USA

www.improveyourlife.net
info@improveyourlife.net

For bulk purchases of this book, please contact the publisher.

To my Mum and Dad

for giving me such a head start

*"Our greatest fear is not that we are weak,
but that we are powerful beyond measure."*

Nelson Mandela

*

*"When you were born, you were soft and supple.
When you die, you will be hard and stiff.*

*Green shoots are fresh and full of vitality.
Dead plants are withered and dry.*

*Hard and stiff go with death.
Soft and supple go with life.*

*An inflexible army never wins a war.
A rigid tree is ready for the axe.*

*The hard and stiff falls,
and the soft and supple rises."*

Tao Te Ching, chapter 76, by Lao Tzu

Acknowledgements

A great many people have played a role in the development of the material contained in this book, and I wish to thank them all. However, I should like to express my especial gratitude to Dr Donald L. Weed, D.C., founder of the Interactive Teaching Method (ITM), who was responsible for formally training me to become a teacher of the Alexander Technique. In the same breath, I should like to thank John Gil, my first Alexander teacher, who introduced me to the teachings of F M Alexander.

I should also like to thank the following Alexander teachers for their on-going support and helpful suggestions during the long process of writing this book:

Emma Jarrett, Regina Neuenhausen, Estella Yu Caldwell, Tim Kjeldsen, Anke Leppke, Ian Traynar and David Horn.

And a very large thank-you goes out to all my students, past and present. A few deserve a special mention, however, not least for persisting with me as their teacher in the early days, when I was experimenting with the structure and content of my introductory ten-week course, and was making even more mistakes than I do now. Thank-you to:

Alex Johns, Erica Handol, Nigel West, Gregor Haska, Anne de Moor, Liz Davis, Rosamund Payne, Evert Wilbrennink, Veronica Pollard, Lynne Cartlidge, Andy Lumborg, Diane Bowler, Adrian Bourner and Kate Brown.

(Some of these people are now well along the way to becoming teachers in their own right.)

I should also like to thank:

Pete Baillee for supporting me to pilot my introductory course and material from this book with drama students at Bristol University.

Kevin Lehane for encouraging me to pilot my introductory course and accompanying material from this book with key personnel at Orange (Mobile Telephone Company) in Bristol.

And also David Scott, Wyn Mason, Ben Cole and Tim Freke for continually challenging my ideas.

A final thankyou to Chloe for not worrying about everything else that needed to be done while I was busy writing.

The Interactive Teaching Method (ITM)

Although the bulk of the material in this book derives from the ITM, the ideas expressed and the manner in which they are expressed are mine, and the book is not to be read as a statement of ITM theory or practice. For that, reader is recommended to read either "What You Think Is What You Get" or "Four Days in Bristol" by Dr Donald L. Weed, D.C..

Note on the use of examples

I have decided to change the names, and in some instance minor incidental details, in order to preserve the anonymity of those students whose stories I relate in what follows.

All Photographs
by Mark Simmons
www.marksimmonsphotography.co.uk
+44 (0)7778 063 699
+44 (0)117 9140 999

Contents

Readying the Ship

*"Change involves carrying out an activity
against the habit of life."*

F·M Alexander

Opening Words

"Begin with the end in mind."
Stephen Covey

First Course

I live in Bristol, a small but vibrant city in the South West of England. Although I wasn't born here, I have lived in Bristol on and off for so long, I have come to think of Bristol as my home.

Bristol is also where I work. It is where I teach and write. What I teach are courses in self-improvement, and in this book I have written the core components of my first course down. In fact, the bulk of this book has evolved from my first course and lends support to the course. But I have also written a stand-alone guide. This book maps out a journey anyone can take to bring about lasting and on-going improvement in their lives.

So my book is about improvement. It is a book about getting better.

But it is also an ideas book. And an action book. Specifically, it is about the relationship between ideas and action, and the principles that govern this all-important relationship in our lives. It is concerned with what we do and how we do it. But even more than that, it is about what we need to change so we can do it better.

And I know we can.

If only… we are willing to change.

I call my first course, "Principles for Improving Your Life," and from time to time I give talks in Bristol to promote it. When I ask people why they have come along to a talk, they cite all sorts of reasons: to improve their health, to gain peace of mind, to walk with more poise, to sing better, because they are curious, because they think there is something wrong with them and I can fix it, because they are keen to move on to something better in their lives. As a rule, it doesn't matter why they have come, only that they have, and that they have come for a reason, that is, there is something they hope to achieve. For, as Bloody Mary sings: "If you haven't got a dream, how you gonna have your dream come true?"[1]

We all need an aspiration, a dream, an ambition; we need a sense of the place we hope to go. Some people call this: having an aim, a goal, a purpose, or even, an end they wish to gain. It can be big or small, grand or frivolous, but it is something you need. Because it is your aspirations that will set your ship sailing, that will suggest a direction for setting out on the voyage.

"If you haven't got a dream, how you gonna have your dream come true?"

South Pacific

Over the years, people have told me they want to sleep better at night, to build a successful business, to write a book, to sing on stage, to be able to laugh again, to be a better person, to help themselves, or their parents, or their children, to forgive, to make amends, to improve their standard of living, to do something about the injustice in the world. There are as many aspirations as there are people. Or so it seems.

But, of much more importance right now is:

"What is it you hope to achieve?"

The other day, a new student, Eve, told me she couldn't answer the what do you hope to achieve question. "Nothing comes to mind," she said. "I have no idea at all."

When students respond in this way, it is seldom the case that they genuinely have no aspirations, but more often that the sense they have of themselves is too vague. Somewhere in the course of their life, they have lost a sense of themselves. When this happens, I recommend they pick a goal. Any goal that comes to mind. If it turns out it was a poor choice, they will find out as the course progresses and then they can change it. That's right, aspirations do not have to remain fixed. In my class, you keep the right to change your mind. In fact, later on I shall argue that acquiring the ability to change course is an essential requirement for getting better. In human affairs, flexibility is a prerequisite for success.

The advice to pick a goal does not work for everyone, however. Once in a while, someone will insist there simply is nothing they could honestly write down. All attempts at identifying goals appear false. If that's you, then the course I recommend is this: make your goal finding your goal. Because you need one, at least if you want to attend my course. It's a qualifying criterion. For if you have no aspirations whatsoever, then we have no reason to begin the voyage.

So: what is it you hope to achieve?[2]

Another Question

"In human affairs, flexibility is a prerequisite for success."

The first question is not the only question. There is another. It relates to something we've already touched upon. And it's this:

"Is it okay if you change?"

Long ago, my primary teacher in the field of self-improvement, Don Weed, asked me this very question. Now I follow and honour him by asking my students the same question:

"Is it okay if you change?"

"But why?" someone will sometimes ask. "Why must I be willing to change?"

You must be willing to change because it's not possible to get better if you stay as you are.

As Stephen Covey quotes Einstein: "the signficant problems we face cannot be solved at the same level of thinking we were at when we created them."[3]. It is madness to believe you can get better if you keep going in the exactly the same way.

Every student, sooner or later, has to realise that they can only get what they want, what they really want, if they are willing to change. They come to see that keeping going as they are now is what is stopping them from getting better. [Often, it is making them worse.] They wake up to the fact that their current way of going about things is the most significant thing standing between them and improvement. They must realise this, because initially at least, for a great many people, that's not how it seems.

"It is madness to believe you can get better if you keep going in exactly the same way."

Many years ago, I attended a performance enhancement workshop, and by the end of the first day I was feeling truly miserable. I had nothing in common with any of the people in the room - as far as I could see - and learning to do something better just wasn't going to change how I felt. I was beginning to wish I had never signed up in the first place. Just then, the presenter looked up from what he was doing and said, "If you don't like it where you are, then move."

"Easy for you say," were the words instantly ringing in my head.

In fact, for a brief paranoid moment, I wondered had he just made this remark to wound me. The idea that what I was doing in that moment had any relation to my perceived suffering struck me as truly absurd. And the fact that the presenter could make such a glib remark was clear proof of his crass insensitivity.

"The significnat problems we face cannot be solved at the same level of thinking we were at when we created them."

Albert Einstein

I didn't like it where I was, but moving wasn't going to help. As far as I could see, my misery had something to do with what was happening around me, with what had happened before, and for that reason it was downright offensive to suggest that I could do something about it by going some place else.

Oh, how things change!

For, if someone were to tell me now that they didn't like it where they were, I might well give them the same advice: "If you don't like it where you are, then move." And for the person who claims not to know how, I might very well recommend they seek out a teacher who can show them.

It may be insensitive, it may sound rude, it may appear to take no account of the very real indignities and suffering that so many people have experienced and continue to experience, no apparent account of the huge obstacles that some people face as they begin the task of getting better, but it is nonetheless true. If you want to get better, either in yourself or in what you do, then you must move. You cannot hope to get better if you stay where you are. What is more, as I shall argue in the next chapter, if you try to stay where you are you will almost certainly get worse.

"Okay, so maybe I do need to change to get better. But change what? What is it I need to change?"

What you need to change are your ideas. In particular, you need to change what I call your guiding ideas, that is, ideas associated with rules governing both what you do and how you do it.

"That's all?"

Yes, that's all you need to do.

In fact, it's all you can do.

As it happens, most of my students tell me they want to change, they are desperate to change, there's nothing in the whole world they long for more, without fully realizing all that changing entails. In fact, if they did, they might not want to attend my course at all, because being willing to change means being willing to give up being the person they currently are. What's worse, they may have to give up the part they are most attached to, which is usually that part which is the source of their woes. In extreme cases, when the change they need to make is profound, this can feel like a matter of life and death.

So: is it? Is it okay if you change?

I hope so, because I want you to go on from here.

"Now just hold on a minute. You said, 'All I need to do to improve is to change my ideas, in particular, my guiding ideas.'"

Yes, I did.

"Well, what on earth does that mean?"

Let me give you some examples to explain.

The other week, I was watching snooker on TV. Like many people who live in Britain, it's a sport I enjoy watching, especially when it's really well-played. On this particular occasion, I was struck by the insight and intelligence of one of the commentators, a certain Willie Thorne. When it came to making decisions about the best way to "go into the reds" to make a high break, he seemed to me to be without equal. Time and again, his predictions about how a cluster of balls would spread according to where and how the cue-ball struck them came true. In my opinion, the man is an undoubted master. He is able to foresee problems and devise creative solutions when break-building other top players do not even seem to consider.

Willie Thorne's mastery of the game is borne out by the fact that, when he still played competitive snooker, rumours abounded that other professionals would not play him privately for money. The risks were too high; his game was too good. But, and this is the real significance of the story, Willie Thorne never got to the very top of the world rankings; he never won the titles everyone else presumed a player of his outstanding ability would. And the reason for his comparative failure, so it is generally agreed, is that Mr Thorne was unable to produce his best when under pressure, something which was especially true when the television cameras were on.

Willie Thorne did not just possess a theoretical ability. His prowess as a world-beating break-builder is well-known. He could demonstrate his mastery outside tournaments by winning game after game against the best players in the world. However, when it mattered, when it mattered most, when it mattered most to Willie Thorne, when he was playing for prestige and not for money, he let himself down. Under extreme pressure he would start to miss balls he would otherwise always pot.

In this regard, Mr Thorne is like many of the people who come to my improvement classes. In life, they all too often under-perform; when it matters, they perform way below their best. In many instances, they have a clear idea about what they want to do, but when faced with an opportunity to put their ideas into action, they seem to lack the necessary control of themselves.

And what I am saying is this: for Willie Thorne, and everyone like him, getting better will involve changing their guiding ideas, that is, the rules governing not only what they do but how they do it.

Or take the case of Cynthia, an accomplished artist, who came to my improvement class last year. Cynthia told me that she had been unable to get the effect she desired when drawing. She wanted a certain ease and freedom of line, qualities she believed her earlier work exemplified, but now seemed to be disappearing from her work. "I know what my problem is," she said. "When I concentrate on my drawing, I tighten the muscles in my fingers, hand and arm. I get so stiff it's impossible for me to draw well."

"Then why don't you stop making yourself stiff?" I innocently asked.

"I can't. Believe me, I try to, but that only makes matters worse. I don't know why, but I just can't stop."

Like Willie, Cynthia too has a problem. In essence, it's much the same problem. Both of these people, for whatever reason, are (at least some of the time) unable to put their ideas into practice. They know what they want to do (or what they want to stop doing), that is, they have a clear idea about what it is they want to change in themselves, but when they get down to it, something in their performance lets them down.

Or let's take the case of Vicky, who is also one of my students. By chance, Vicky is an artist too. Some time ago, Vicky told me the following story.

Vicky had gone to have lunch with a friend. During the meal, Vicky found herself talking about a problem she was having. Basically, every time a potential buyer came to her studio and said something approving about one of her paintings, Vicky didn't believe them. "They're just saying that to be nice," she would think. As a result, if the potential buyer enquired about the price of the painting, Vicky would look embarrassed and say it wasn't for sale.

The friend said, "I know what that is. It's a cognitive distortion. It's when you discount any facts that cause you to revise your negative view of yourself. It's called discounting the positive. It's a faulty way of thinking. It's based on a wrong idea." Vicky's friend smiled, confident she had solved the problem. But to her surprise, Vicky said, "I know it's a cognitive distortion. But knowing it doesn't help. I still keep reacting in the same old way."

"They have a clear idea about what it is they want to change in themselves, but when they get down to it, something in their performance lets them down."

The idea of cognitive distortions in relation to how we see ourselves is powerful. Identifying cognitive distortions can be used as a mighty tool for change. It's what I like to call a good idea. However, for Vicky, in that moment, the tool alone was insufficient. She lacked the wherewithal to use it. She found herself unable to act as if this good idea were true.

There are many, many books full of good ideas. Indeed, I will draw your attention to a fair number in the course of writing this one. Very few, however, concern themselves with the business of putting ideas into practice, especially when the instrument of their use is ourselves. In that regard, this book is different, for in this book I will address the issue of getting better by learning how to improve the relationship between ideas and action in our selves.

Regrettably, for far too many people, being told what to do to improve is insufficient, as they lack the wherewithal to make the best of themselves. They may be told, or even figure out for themselves, the best way of swinging a golf-club, giving a presentation, being a parent, sitting in a chair, writing a book, or running a business, but when they actually get down to it, something in their performance lets them down. They fail to deliver their best ideas. For whatever reason, they fall short of their full potential.

In the chapters that follow, I will address this vitally important issue by describing a technique for improving our ability to successfully translate our ideas into deeds. I will do this by outlining principles which, when consciously and consistently applied, have the power to generate on-going and lasting improvements in our general standard of performance, irrespective of the task with which we are engaged.

And if you are tempted to make this journey with me, if you are minded to follow the path I shall be mapping out, then what I am claiming is this: you must be willing to change, in particular, to change what I am calling your guiding ideas.

So it all boils down to two simple questions:

Do you aspire? And: Are you willing to change?

One of my aspirations is to fashion a life of contribution, in which I make a difference in a constructive and lasting way. And I am willing to change. Oh, from time to time, you'll find me wandering the streets of Bristol fighting tooth and nail to resist the changes I need to make, but, the intention is there. I aspire and I am willing to change. And that's all it takes.... to get on my course.

So, if that's you, if you have a dream and are willing to change to reach it, then read on. If, however, you are happy as you are, and have no aspirations in the direction of improvement, then close the book now and give it to a friend. For the ideas in this book are expanding. And, if you choose to consciously and consistently apply them, you will change your life. You will make it bigger. And better. You will go forward. In spite of yourself. You will advance. And that's because, as F M

"When all that is important has been said in favour of good thoughts, ideas, systems and methods... the real problem - the practical application of the concepts - remains unsolved."

F M Alexander

"The lack of real happiness manifested by the majority of adults today is due to the fact that they are experiencing not an improving, but a continually deteriorating use of their psycho-physical selves."

F M Alexander

Alexander wrote, "Expanding ideas are the forerunners of human advancement."[4]

I happen to agree. But if you don't, then so much the better. It is for people like you I am writing this book.

Taking the First Step

In 1991, I made my first ever trip to America. I flew from London to New York and on to San Francisco.

On my first day in California, I saw the Golden Gate Bridge, a mighty construction suspended across the mouth of the Bay. This beautiful bridge, radiant in the California sunshine, is painted a deep, rusty red[5]; it connects the city of San Francisco to Marin County in the North. I was reminded of home, for just a few miles from Bristol is the Severn Bridge, another colossal suspension bridge, in this instance spanning the Severn Estuary, thereby joining England to Wales. The Severn Bridge, by contrast, is painted off-white, no doubt to blend more easily with our frequently cloudy skies.[6]

"Expanding ideas are the forerunners of human advancement."

F M Alexander

It occurred to me that no one in San Francisco would know that in Bristol itself, spanning the Avon Gorge, was the Clifton Suspension Bridge, one of the first ever suspension bridges to be built. It was designed in 1831 by Isambard Kingdom Brunel, and soon became the prototype for all the colossal suspension bridges we see in the world today. Brunel said that he wanted to prove to his doubting colleagues that it was possible to build a suspension bridge across such a wide span. In the event, he was proven right, for his bridge opened to traffic in 1864, five years after his death, and fifteen years after the California goldrush.

I had often walked across the Clifton Suspension Bridge, spanning as it does the deep Avon Gorge, and wondered how they ever managed to build it. For the bulk of the bridge seems to hang in mid air; there appears to be no way that during its construction it could have been supported from below. 'How did they do that?' I wondered.

The answer, I discovered, was with a kite and a piece of string. So legend has it, the cunning Brunel attached a thin piece of string to a kite and flew the kite high in the air. The kite was eventually caught by someone standing on the other side. And from that single piece of string spanning the gorge, Brunel was able to thread across another, and another, and another, till he could finally send across a rope. And from a single rope came two ropes then three ropes, till finally they had so many ropes going from one side to the other, he could tie them together and hang them from mighty brick towers built on either side. These ropes were so strong that he could attach to these ropes heavy steel ropes, and from these heavier metal ropes suspend the first girders. In this way, from a single piece of string, he began to construct a mighty bridge of stone and steel.

"Just as every journey begins with a single step, so the accomplishment of every dream begins with a single idea."

In the course of my life, I have often been called upon or chosen to undertake challenges that initially seemed beyond me. 'I could never do that,' I remember telling myself. Whether it was writing a book, raising a child, singing in public, or getting over the loss of someone I loved: 'I'll never do that,' I remember hearing myself say. These days, when faced with challenges that seem beyond me, I am more likely to recall the story of the Clifton Suspension Bridge. I will think of Brunel flying his kite.

If you want to make a change, if the change you want to make is big, I now know you do not have to do it all at once. Like Brunel, I can start with something small. I can start with a single piece of string. As a consequence, whenever I teach my improvement classes I remind myself that no matter who the student, no matter how big the change they need to make to fulfil their aspiration, everyone can start with something small.

Just as every journey begins with a single step, so the accomplishment of every dream begins with a single idea. And the idea does not even need to be original. All that is required is that it works.

"So your book is all about ideas, is that what you're saying? It's a book for intellectuals, right?"

No. It's a book for people interested in improvement; it's for people who aspire to get better. Above all, it's practical. It's about the practical application of ideas. It is a book about the life you're living now. And how to engage with ideas that will change it for the better. The reason it focuses on ideas, specifically your guiding ideas, is because it is these ideas that drive your actions. And if you disagree, then do, please, read on a while more. I've got plenty to say to you. And to just about everyone else who wants to improve.

So, despite the emphasis on ideas, I have not written a philosophical treatise, but rather a how-to book on the application of good ideas. And the ideas in it work. They have been road-tested by me, by my students, by my teachers and my colleagues, and by countless others who have made journeys of their own. And if you take the trouble to understand and apply them, they will work for you. You can make your life better. You can improve.

You may be reassured to know that I have had the privilege of teaching these principles to students, teachers, engineers, environmentalists, musicians, actors, artists, alternative health-care practitioners, mainstream health-care practitioners, academics, business-people, unemployed people and countless sundry others. They have been young, old and in-between. They have been rich and poor, lived in bodies of different shapes and sizes, and had different coloured skins. Most could walk and talk easily, but not all. Most were in reasonably good health, but not all. Some were sent by their employers, or their spouses, but the overwhelming majority came of their own accord. And in every single case, when the student took the trouble to work the ideas, the ideas have worked for them. Everyone can get better; everyone can improve.

The Teachings of F M Alexander

My course, "Principles for Improving Your Life," has a sub-title. It is this: "inspired by the teachings of F M Alexander."

If that comes as a surprise, let me explain.

It is my sincere conviction that in the teachings of F M Alexander I have found the most effective and powerful tools for getting better I will ever likely find. In all my searching, I have never come across anything more practical, more persuasive, more relevant, as the principles he articulated and put to work.

"But why F M Alexander? Surely he doesn't have a monopoly on good ideas?"

No, of course not. I for one do not believe any one person or school of thought has a monopoly on good ideas. My two main reasons for basing my courses on the teachings of F M Alexander are these:

One: During his long and productive life, F M Alexander actually devised a means for improving our ability to translate our ideas into action. In his books, he calls that means his technique. It is a practical method for bringing about on-going and lasting improvements in whatever it is we do.

Two: F M Alexander was one of the first people to recognise the profound signficance for human-beings of living in a rapidly changing environment. The technique he developed derived from a recognition of what's involved in not only surviving but thriving in a changing world. His technique can help us to generate that flexibility in thought and action necessary to become and stay well in changing times.

F M Alexander

To that extent, if we are interested in getting better, the teachings of F M Alexander are simply too important to ignore.

So my book is about improvement. It is a book about getting better. But it is also about the work of F M Alexander. I have written it to provide you with a solid foundation for learning his technique. It is based on my ten-week introductory course, which in turn is based upon an assignment I was set during my training to become a teacher of F M Alexander's technique. It is an assignment I have done over and over again since: namely, to identify the ten most important principles in the teachings of F M Alexander, and to rank them in order of importance.

Over time, I have come to see that the best sequence for arranging the principles depends on the task at hand; it is not a question of one solution for every problem, but rather, the best tools for the job at hand; and in sequencing them here I have been guided by my belief in the order that it is best for most students to learn them and for me to teach them. To that end, I have chosen a sequence that makes sense to me. I have sought to lay a foundation before starting the walls. I have put off laying the roof till after the walls were done.

So that is what I offer here: a series of principles for improvement; a sequence of rules for getting better. The sequence I have chosen is important, in that if you follow it you will find a simple and coherent path-way to follow. But the sequence is not fixed. For another purpose, I might well want to arrange them differently.

I should say that the principles in this book are not the only principles in Mr Alexander's work, but they are central to his work. For that reason, I do not intend what I have written to be viewed as the be-all and end-all on Mr Alexander's technique. No, what I have written is simply an introductory guide, that is, a set of tools and sign-posts for getting better. There are, however, other accounts that portray his work differently, as if it were sensory awareness training, or body work, or even an alternative medicine. In my view, nothing could be further from the truth. So, if what I say conflicts with what you have already heard, then please don't worry yourself unduly. Even if what I am saying seems horribly wrong, it may simply be that my reasons are not immediately apparent.

Before moving on, I should also like to point out that everything I claim in this book is based on tested experience. I claim nothing for which I do not have compelling reasons to believe. That said, may I stress again that I do not intend what I have written to be treated as truths carved in stone; rather, as a set of keys that will open doors, or well-hoisted sails that will help you change to a better course, that will give you the practical means to bring about improvements in whatever it is you do.

A Note of Caution

The following aphorism was coined by F M Alexander:

"Be careful of the printed matter. You may not read it as it is written down."[7]

This advice is especially apt when reading material that seeks to express new ideas. People are wont to rush headlong towards conclusions before they have surveyed sufficient of the ground to reach a fair appraisal. All too often, they imagine the author must be saying this or that, according to what they have read in books of this type before.

"Be careful of the printed matter. You may not read it as it is written down."

F M Alexander

When making this claim, I really do speak from direct personal experience. I will hold up my hand and confess that I, like so many of my colleagues, students and friends, on first reading F M Alexander, washed over passages that made little appeal, focusing instead on those that did, in the process twisting my interpretation to conform to my preconceived ideas. I knew what he was saying, even though much of it made little sense, even though his language was unfamiliar and arcane.

In this book, I anticipate that I will be presenting many new ideas, as well as many old ones, and to that extent you may find F M Alexander's advice useful to bear in mind: "Beware of the printed matter. You may not read it as it is written down."

The other day, my son, Leif, was playing a game on my computer. There were patterns of numbers and shapes in a row, and he had to predict the next number or shape in the sequence.

For example:

1   3   5   ?

The way I saw it, he was developing a useful skill. We all need to be able to recognise patterns to make sense of our world. This skill, however, when called upon in a mechanical, unthinking way, can severely limit our ability to apprehend what is actually going on in a particular case. For example, what if someone wished to present sequences like these:

1   3   5   3   1   3   5

In these cases, three or four shapes or numbers would be insufficient to make a sound judgement about how the sequence continued. So it is with books expressing new ideas.

Time and again, when I have begun to describe what I teach on my improvement courses, before I have introduced more than the first three or four ideas, people have said: "I get it - what you're saying is it's a case of mind over matter," or, "So you're saying I need to replace bad habits with good ones," or, "It's just like positive thinking; I just need to think more positively," or, "So you teach people how to relax." The list goes on.

In each case, as far as I was concerned, I had said nothing of the sort. The interpretation reached came from a decision to match what I was teaching to an idea the person brought to the table from their past experience of how courses like mine worked.

So let me make the following plea: Hold back from jumping to too quick a conclusion! You might be pleasantly surprised.

A Little More About Me

In the pages that follow I hope to share with you what it is I have come to know, the many things I have learned along the way, that have changed my life for the better. But before I do, I'd like to say a few words about my life before I ever heard of F M Alexander and his widely acclaimed, if little understood, technique.

I first heard of F M Alexander in the Winter of 1995. Back then, I was spending lots of time running my own business, Groups In Learning, or Gil, as it was known. Curiously, given that I was about to begin a period of profound personal transformation, Gil was a rip-roaring success. In fact, everything in my life seemed to be going well, even if, below the surface, I knew there was trouble brewing.

I had set up Gil in 1992 as a one-man training and consultancy service offering personal and professional development courses. In the main, it was work that interested me; it was work I enjoyed. But, by the end of 1994, I couldn't help notice that a new and unwelcome trend had begun to set in; the more work I did, the more I sensed I was losing touch with myself, with what I would have called my inner self. A clear symptom of this was my finding it increasingly difficult to write fiction, something I had always wanted to do, and something I had been working at on and off for the last several years. At the ripe old age of 31, I had the feeling that I was losing the freedom, the spontaneity, the vitality of my youth. Increasingly, I found myself unable to run training courses and then to write. For the first time, I was unable to make the two things work together.

At about the same time, I was being offered more and more drugs education training, something I had plenty of experience of from a previous job, but a topic that, in all honesty, I no longer wanted to teach. This presented me with a quandary. I didn't want to turn the new business away, but my real interest, so far as Gil was concerned, was in running the development courses.

In the event, I opted for the following compromise. I would run my development courses whenever opportunities arose, but for now I'd accept offers to do drugs education training. For a while, all went well with this plan; I did a mixture of both types of course. The bills got paid and I got job-satisfaction. However, such was the demand for drugs education training that I soon found myself hiring an administrator and then renting an office to house her; next, I sub-contracted freelance trainers to train with and finally for me; in the end, I was employing staff to run their own drugs education training courses.

By 1995, it certainly seemed like I was running a successful business and enjoying the associated privileges. At work, I was the boss, which, having not always enjoyed being line-managed in the past, suited me fine. At home, I lived in an elegant city-centre flat with my girl-friend, Chloe, and we enjoyed the city's finest views. In addition, I now had the money to travel to America and Crete, where friends lived with whom I wanted to stay in touch. But, somehow in this changed and changing world I was no longer happy. At the end of each successful course - and they were highly successful - I couldn't escape noticing that instead of the usual high, I felt flat, empty, drained; and not just the drug education training, but all of the courses I ran. Worse, the more work I did, the harder I found it engage my imagination. I was getting myself into a particular mind-set to go to work, and then, afterwards, when I wanted a different one to write, I could no longer shake the first one off. My writing self and my working self were no longer able to co-exist. On bad days, I figured I'd have to abandon Gil altogether if I was ever to write well again.

Something I couldn't put my finger on was definitely going wrong with me. I needed something in my life to change, but I couldn't see what, or, on those days when I thought I could, how.

This, then, was the backdrop to my life when I happened to notice a poster in a newsagents window announcing a group class in the Alexander Technique. I had no interest in learning the Alexander Technique, which I assumed was about standing up with a straight back so you could sing better, but it did occur to me I'd like to be in someone else's group, that is, not be the person running it. For a couple of hours a week, for the next few weeks, I could take some time for me. What's more, I reasoned, I was bound to learn something from watching someone else approach the task of running the group; no doubt I'd find some teaching tool I could later use myself. In fact, attending the group would be like sending a signal to the Universe that I was going to start running more of my own groups, on topics other than drugs education. "Yes," I said to myself, almost carrying myself away, "I will sign up!" But - there almost always is one - I was busy, extremely busy, and did I really want to waste time sitting in a cold room in a community centre listening to someone rabbit on about how to sit and stand properly? Of course not, no.

And yet, as I stood there gazing at the poster, there was something that kept drawing my attention. What was it? And then it clicked: it was the name of the man running the group: John Gil! He had the same name as my business. I dug my hands deeper in my pockets and pulled my coat tighter, giving myself a few moments to mull over the role coincidence had played in life, (and how much I preferred my Winters in California), when it occurred to me that I hadn't allowed myself to act on the basis of a presumed message from the Universe to me for years, in fact, probably not since launching Gil in the first place. And so, in a fit of something out of my ordinary, I wrote down John's telephone number and walked on, resolved to attend his course.

Two weeks later I showed up for the first class. A group of about seven of us were sitting in a semi-circle on plastic chairs. John, our teacher, had just begun introducing himself, when all of a sudden a distraught woman burst into the room with a five-year old girl. Apparently, the baby-sitter had let her down but she was coming anyway and there was nothing that could be done and she was here now and she didn't want to miss the class and... She looked at John, seemingly ready to pounce on him or burst into tears if he hinted that she and her daughter might not be welcome in his class.

Now, as someone used to running groups, I was more than a little curious to see how Mr Gil would fare. I knew from my own experience of training people that the one thing you could count on was that not everything would go to plan. Direct personal experience of training and hiring others to train had taught me that a person's ability to respond to the unexpected was a useful guide to their ability to run a course well.

In the event, John barely reacted at all. He welcomed the woman and her child. He asked the girl if she would like to sit with her Mum or do some colouring at the back of the room. The child chose colouring and Mum joined the group. And then we moved on. There was no fussing, no delay, no fluster. John's response had been simple, direct, clear. He easily returned to the point where he had been interrupted. I was silently impressed.

After his welcome, John asked us if we had any questions. John impressed me again. Only someone confident of their abilities to respond in the moment throws the floor open to a new class. Also, by asking us if we had any questions John was signalling to us that our concerns and issues were important to him. In terms of my values, John was doing just fine.

Next, John wrote up a definition on a board:

The Alexander Technique

is the

study

of

thinking

in relation to

movement.[8]

For me, that was something of a surprise. I had thought the Alexander Technique has something to do with body posture. "Thinking" was the last thing on my mind. I put up my hand. "Is that the only definition?" I asked.

"No," said John with a smile. There were other definitions, other ideas, but this was the best definition he knew, and over the coming weeks he would have an opportunity to explain to me why. Another good answer. I wanted to find out more.

And so, in a community centre in South Bristol, in the Winter of 1995, I began my own journey of discovery into the little-known world of F M Alexander's technique. Unlike many who get involved in the business of change, I was in no especial pain. I was experiencing neither physical nor mental collapse. There was no immediate divorce, nor bereavement, nor loss of job. I just had a growing sense that I was no longer going the right way. And that if I kept going as I was, my situation was likely to get worse.

John Gil teaching.

I had no out-of-this-world experience during my first class. I just felt more comfortable, more relaxed. But something had begun. Something had been achieved. Questions had formulated inside me. In particular, I wanted to know if John's way of working with the group had anything to do with the ideas he was teaching, or was it some ability he had picked up independently by himself. It never occurred to me then that the so-called problems I was having in sorting out what I was doing with my life would find a solution in the ideas he was presenting.

And now, a little more than seven years later, I may not be able to put all my good ideas into practice, and I certainly don't profess to have all of life's problems solved, but I am at last back on the right track.

Increasingly, I find the courage to act on my convictions, and the wherewithal to live the life I've only secretly dreamed of in the past. I am learning to discard "I can't" and to embrace "I haven't yet"; I am discovering the confidence to walk into a new and exciting unknown. I am writing fiction again; and, I no longer feel empty after a good days work. All in all, I am getting better.

A Word on the Structure of This Book

The next chapter is all about F M Alexander. I have written it to provide you with useful background information for learning his technique. It includes a brief biographical account along with an introduction to some of his basic discoveries and ideas.

The next ten chapters each address a core principle. I have based these chapters on what I teach in my introductory course. Ordinarily, people would engage with this material (the first time round) over a period of ten weeks.

I would ask that you read each of these chapters in the light of whatever it is you hope to achieve, that is, that you consider the principles outlined in relation to your aspiration.

These ten chapters, taken as a whole, outline a journey. They are not to be read as distinct units that bear no relation to each other, but rather as links in a chain, or rungs up a ladder, or stepping stones across a river you hope to cross. You may find that the destination you have in mind does not come into plain view till near the end. If this happens, please remember that this is the case in many journeys we take in life. Just because we can't see our chosen destination from the outset, this does not mean we are going the wrong way.

The first three principles establish a foundation for bringing about on-going improvements in everything you do. Work through these and you give yourself the best possible grounding for reaching your chosen goal.

In chapters four, five and six, I outline principles that relate to pitfalls or holes in the road. I call this section, Navigating Reefs and Rocks. Here, I deal with the ways most people go wrong by doing anything but building on the foundations they have laid. In my view, it is a mistake to avoid them. Taking time here will save you much work and aggravation as you press on.

In chapter 7 we return to the beginning once more, to check the course you have charted. Here, you will have an opportunity to re-consider the appropriateness of the steps you are taking in light of the destination you seek.

In the eighth, ninth and tenth chapters you will encounter tools that will help you to build on the foundation and avoid the pit-falls, to enable you to make your good ideas become real. In the very last chapter, I address the issue of putting it all together, that is, what it means to work to principle in the living of your life.

So, here it is, my book of getting better: Principles for Improving Your Life.[9]

Notes

1. From the Musical, *South Pacific*.

2. At the beginning of the course, I am happy for students to answer the *what do you hope to achieve* question pretty much anyhow they please. Only the person — usually the one who has had previous lessons in the Alexander Technique — who insists it is wrong to have aspirations, that we should live our lives without having an end in mind, is likely to run aground here. So long as the student has an aim, however tiny, original, fantastical, or plain, I don't really care.

So long as there is something they want to achieve, and they are genuinely prepared to change to reach it, then we have a basis to proceed.

This does not mean that success is guaranteed, but it does mean we have a basis to proceed. For me, if how the student goes about achieving their goal has a bearing on success or failure, then I have reason to suppose I might be able to help. I may be wrong, but I do have a sound basis to proceed.

As the course progresses, however, I will sometimes invite students to frame their aspiration in such a way that they can enhance the chances of eventual success.

Let me explain.

Some people frame their aspirations in such a way that they significantly increase their difficulties before they even get started. They do this by framing goals in such a way that success is almost impossible, or success is beyond the scope of their personal influence, or their goal is so vague that no one could tell whether or not they'd succeeded.

Consider the following:

"My goal is to live forever."

"I want my partner to stop smoking cigarettes."

"I intend to improve."

Now consider these:

"My goal is to live a long and productive life. Therefore I aim to stay fit in mind and body by keeping mentally and physically active."

"I aim to do what I can to arouse in my partner an eager desire to quit smoking."

"By next Summer, I hope to be good enough to pass the practical exam."

Now ask yourself: which of these aspirations would you rather teach? If you had to figure out a pathway to go from where the student is now to where they hope to go, which set of aspirations would you choose?

For me, the choice is clear.

We can make reaching our destination easier by framing our destination with care.

We can choose something achievable (which does not exclude ambitious).

We can choose something over which we have influence.

We can choose something tangible and clear.

So: "What do you hope to achieve?"

3. pg 42, *The Seven Habits of Highly Effective People* by Stephen Covey.

4. pg 13, *Constructive Conscious Control of the Individual* by F M Alexander.

5. The colour is known as International Orange.

6. Since then, a second bridge has been built to cope with the ever-increasing traffic.

7. From *Notes of Instruction* in *The Alexander Technique - the essential writings of F M Alexander* selected by Ed Maisel.

8. This definition is attributed to Dr Connie Amundson of Seattle, who offered it in response to a quiz set her by Don Weed.

9. I teach my first course as follows:

Each week I begin by asking my students if they have any questions, or observations, or thoughts to share. Then I introduce a principle, usually by giving a presentation, telling a story, making a demonstration, or reading aloud some text. Then I work with students on self-chosen activities. This enables me to demonstrate the application of the principle in question, or a different one, according to the issues that are generated.

During this last year, activities have included (among others): sitting, standing, walking, jogging, running, juggling, singing, dancing, playing guitar, cello, violin, harp, playing golf, cycling, yoga, Tai Chi, shaving, brushing teeth, sandwich making, giving a presentation, answering questions, speaking French, improvising, acting, reading aloud prose, poetry, Shakespeare, getting dressed, getting undressed, going to sleep, getting up, and even carrying a baby.

Frederick Matthias Alexander

"You translate everything,
whether physical or mental or spiritual,
into muscular tension."
F M Alexander[1]

F M Alexander: His Story[2]

F M Alexander - F M to his intimates - was born in 1869 in Tasmania, just off the coast of mainland South Eastern Australia. He grew up on the family farm with his many brothers and sisters, and was educated at the local school; and also at home, for it seems the young F M was often poorly, and regularly confined to his bed.

F M tells us that as a boy he had a love of poetry and the plays of Shakespeare, and he would spend long hours attempting to interpret the characters. It was this passion that led the young F M, aged 17, now working as a clerk in the office of a tin-mine, to take up amateur dramatics. In fact, such was F M's enthusiasm for the dramatic arts that he began a study of every branch of dramatic expression, with a view to becoming a professional actor. By the age of 22, F M had begun to realize his dream. He was touring Australia and New Zealand, giving one-man recitals of poetry, short stories and soliloquies from Shakespeare. (Shylock and Hamlet were among his favourites, so we are told). And then F M developed a problem. A serious

"You cannot, at the very beginning of our work, have any conception of the evil that results from muscular spasms and physical contraction."

Constantin Stanislavski

problem. It was a problem with his voice.

F M was becoming hoarse when reciting, and his problem was getting worse. Alarmed, F M sought professional and medical advice. For he knew that if he failed to solve his problem, his dreams of an illustrious career as a actor would be dashed. But nothing anyone said or did was helping. F M began to believe there was something wrong with him. One medical adviser agreed. He recommended surgery; he wanted to operate on F M's vocal chords.

F M's own doctor, however, suggested rest. He encouraged F M to give up using his voice altogether. Miraculously, F M's voice began to heal. F M tells us that he followed this advice for two weeks before a particularly important engagement, and, to his immense relief, on the night of the recital, his voice was restored to full health. But - and this must have been especially painful to F M - half-way through the show he could barely utter a word. His voice was worse than ever. Poor F M must have been in the depths of despair.

F M Alexander began a life-long study into the relationship between thinking *and* movement.

The next day, F M tells us, he went to see his doctor. He now believed that rest was no cure at all, since the moment he started to recite his hoarseness had returned. At best, rest was only temporary relief. It was then, sitting in the doctor's surgery, that F M did something remarkable: he put on his thinking cap and took a decision.

The young Frederick Matthias Alexander reasoned as follows: if resting my voice restores it, and reciting ruins it, then it must be something that I am doing when I recite that is causing my problem. F M tells us he shared this reasoning with his doctor. The doctor agreed. "So what is it I am doing?" F M demanded. The doctor confessed he had no idea. "Then I will find out for myself," said F M.

And so began a journey, an epic voyage of historic proportions. For in that moment of decision Alexander began a life-long investigation. What started out as the comparatively simple matter of investigating the mechanics of vocal production, a topic presumably Alexander knew well, soon led him to consider a question that he, and presumably no one before him, had even considered as a possible question to ask: namely, how did he get himself to do what he did? By what processes did he direct himself in activity? F M Alexander began a life-long study into what we call, in the ITM, the relationship between thinking and movement. Alexander wanted to know how and why he was sending himself wrong, and what he could do to stop it. And Alexander found answers. Wonderful answers. Answers full of wonder and surprise. Along the way he discovered things. He invented things. He pointed a way for anyone wanting to follow in his tracks.

An Important Discovery

Alexander had asked his doctor, "What am I doing when I recite?" The doctor confessed he no idea. So Alexander set about finding out for himself. To do this, he first made use of a mirror.

When Alexander watched himself recite in front of the mirror he noticed that he pulled his head back and down, which was also associated with a tendency to depress his larynx and gasp in air. These tendencies were also present in ordinary speaking, but to a much lesser degree, so much so Alexander had not noticed them when he first looked.

Next, something remarkable happened. Alexander discovered that if he succeeded in preventing this pulling back and down of his head as he began to recite, he indirectly checked the depressing of the larynx and the gasping in of air. What is more, when he did this, his condition of hoarseness tended to disappear. For the young Frederick Matthias Alexander, this would later prove to be a profound and significant discovery.

Enthused by the prospect of improving his voice still further, Alexander continued to experiment. In time, F M came to see that his misuse of his head and neck, in conjunction with his misuse of his vocal and breathing organs, was synchronized with a misuse of other parts of his body, including his hands, legs and feet. These misuses involved a condition of undue muscle tension throughout his body. Finally, Alexander came to the shocking but illuminating realisation that the pattern of misuse he had discovered was common to all his activities, not just the act of reciting. Alexander would later call this his habitual manner of use.

Alexander had come a long way. He had solved the problem of vocal production from a mechanical point of view. He had figured out the optimal conditions for using his voice. In order to bring these improved conditions about, he needed to prevent his habitual misuse of himself. And he knew this misuse was associated with his tendency to pull his head back and down. So, if he could just prevent this pulling of his head back and down, surely he could begin to prevent his general misuse of himself. Alexander went to work. He tried to put his discoveries in to practice. But he came unstuck. To his dismay, he found that his habit of pulling his head back and down did not go away simply because he decided it should. And it is largely because Alexander discovered that he could not put his new plan into operation that he went on to develop his technique.

But why couldn't F M put this simple plan into practice? Why can't so many of us? Alexander tells us that he was forced to consider the previously unconsidered question of the direction of the use of himself. That is, what processes was he using to direct himself in activity? And, more to the point, could they be changed? Could they be changed so that he was able to get the results he wanted?

The answer to that question proved to be an emphatic yes. He could in fact change the way he directed himself in activity. He could stop sending himself wrong.

Alexander did so by changing his ideas. He figured out and then worked to a new set of rules. And as he did so, he got better. He improved. Not just in his reciting, but in all kinds of ways. His voice improved, his health improved. He enjoyed an ever-increasing standard of co-ordination* in everything he did; he got better mentally and physically. Over time, he began to acquire what he would later call, "a complete control of his potentialities"[3]; his general standard of performance gradually but steadily improved.

"But what has all this to do with me?" you might think.

Lots... Lots and lots.

Alexander began to study people: his friends, his acting colleagues, people who passed him on the street. And he saw the same wrong uses in others that he had seen in himself. Over time, he was led to conclude that certain wrong uses of the body were always associated with a diminishment in a person's *general* standard of co-ordination. What is more, these wrong uses were always associated with an interference with the right working of the head in relation to the neck, and the head and neck in relation to the torso, caused by undue muscular tension.** And in every single case, an interference in the optimal working of these "primary" relationships was associated with a deterioration in a person's general standard of co-ordination in activity. The more a person interfered, the less they were able to bridge the gap between ideas and action in themselves; the less able were they to make their good ideas become real.

I am well aware that, for many readers, what I have just written may seem hugely problematic or at the very least paradoxical. How can a change in seemingly purely physical relationships – referred to succinctly and quite brilliantly by Don Weed as "the

"It is not the position of the head to the body that matters, rather the dynamic relationship (poise) of head to body."

---

*   When I speak of Alexander's general standard of co-ordination in this context, I am referring to his ability to direct himself in activity according to his wishes.

**   Many beginning students mistakenly believe that Alexander's discovery relates to the position of the head, neck and torso. However, this is not so. For what matters here is how the head moves with respect to the trunk (i.e. relationships), and not where the head and trunk are (i.e. positions). I shall have more to say about this later.

poise of the head in relation to the body"[4] - effect a change in a person's general standard of performance? Or, as one of my readers put it, "I can see how the poise of the head in relation with the body might affect my walking, but my ability to solve a maths problem, surely not?"

In response, let me begin by saying this. Most people have never consciously considered how they get themselves to perform tasks, whether so called physical actions, like walking, or so-called mental actions, like maths. Apart from things like "concentrating" or "focussing their attention," most people perform the numerous acts of everyday life in whatever way feels right. However, as I shall argue in the next chapter, every single activity, whether solving a maths problem or going for a walk, whether composing a piece of music or washing the dishes, involves the inter-dependent working of both 'physical' and 'mental' processes. And this particular relationship (the poise of the head in relation to the body) speaks to their co-ordinated, inter-dependent working. For whatever reason, it tells us about a person's general standard of co-ordination in activity. In this way, it functions as an indicator, or guide.[5,6]

The poise of the head in relation with the body tells us about a person's general standard of co-ordination in activity.

Regarding this, you may be interested to know that one of my students, on hearing of this controversy, said:

"I can see all too clearly how someone could get so anxious at the thought of having to solve a maths problem that they could no longer think straight, and that this tension would express itself as a change in the poise of their head in relation to the body. Of course, I can see that, as that's what I do myself; and if only I could learn how to stop this tensing then I'd be better able to think clearly and thus improve my ability to do maths, but walking? How could a change in the poise of the head in relation to the body affect your ability to walk?"

The more a person interfered, the less they were able to bridge the gap between ideas and action in themselves.

The solution to this particular paradox lies in the word "indicator" or "guide". For what I am claiming is that the nature of this relationship, in any given case, tells us about the way that individual is organising themselves to perform an activity. So that, by observing this particular relationship, we have a way we can make a fair judgment of a person's general standard of co-ordination, and thus, by extension, we have a marvellous tool for gauging a person's progress on the voyage.

In his own case, F M Alexander discovered that once he had learned how to control this relationship in himself, he was able to elevate his general standard of performance in all his activities, and thus bring about improvements in everything he did.

However, before I go on, it is vitally important that I stress that Alexander did not claim he learned to control this relationship directly, in the sense of exerting some specific muscular control. No, the solution Alexander actually put forward, the one that led him to move towards gaining a complete control of his potentialities, was to change the way he did things, so that his approach to the various acts of life became consistent with principles he had reasoned out. For when Alexander changed the way he went about his business, when he changed what he sometimes referred to as his *thinking in activity*, he found that he could in fact stop interfering with the optimum working of these primary relationships, and thus enjoy a constantly improving standard of co-ordination in everything he did. And so can you.

Alexander changed the way he did things so that his approach to the various acts of life became consistent with principles he had reasoned out.

*

Once, on one of those rare occasions when I strayed from Bristol to give my introductory talk further afield, I had just finished introducing this important discovery of F M Alexander when someone raised a hand to object.

"You said, 'I believe' and, 'It seems to be the case that...'. Well, that's not very scientific. It's not very convincing. Can't you do better than that?"

What a good question, I thought. 'Can't you do better than that?' It got me wondering. Could I, or someone at least, prove the truth or falsity of this idea? And what's more, what would count as proof? Might we find a counter-example? Might scientists be able to establish Alexander's discovery as a scientific law?

Unfortunately, I was forced to conclude that answers to these questions were beyond the scope of an introductory talk. Also, they are beyond the scope of this book. However, if you are interested in pursuing the matter further, there are many scientists who have in fact investigated these issues, and I can direct you to their work. In this regard, you may find the observations of one of the twentieth centuries leading biologist's, G. E. Coghill, particularly interesting. For a flavour of his work, Frank Pierce Jones, an esteemed Alexander teacher trained by F M (and his brother A R), quotes Dr Coghill's biographer, C. Judson Herrick:

"Movement, said Coghill, was integrated from the start, with the "total pattern" of the head and trunk dominating the "partial patterns" of the limbs."[8]

(For further information, please refer to the Notes at the end of this chapter.[9])

So, do I *know* that the poise of the head in relation to the body is a reliable indicator of a person's general standard of co-ordination in activity? Can I *prove* it? No - I can only cite evidence in support.

However, I can use Alexander's discovery for myself and when I teach. I can keep it in mind when I go to work and see what happens. And when I do, I have always seen that improvements in the poise of the head in relation with the body in movement have been associated with improvements in a person's *general* standard of co-ordination; no matter what activity they were engaged in; no matter whether they were going for a walk, or playing piano, or articulating an idea.

In practice, for many people, a demonstration on their own person - in some instances many times over – is required before they can grasp the real significance of Alexander's discovery. (For this, they will likely need a teacher. If you would like to make contact with one, please refer to contact information at the end of the book.)

Whether or not it will one day be possible to prove scientifically one way or the other the truth or falsity of Alexander's discovery, the more pertinent issue facing you and me is whether or not we can put it to use. Because, in the final analysis, if we want to improve the way we direct ourselves in activity and thus enjoy greater success in every area of our lives, Alexander's discovery by itself is useless. We must have some practical means of applying his discovery for ourselves.

*

But let's go back to Australia. Alexander sensed he was onto something important. He continued to observe the people around him. He continued to make as detailed a study as he could. Before long, he came to the shocking realisation that everyone else was like him in that they were all - more or less - interfering with the co-ordinated use of themselves. Some more, some less, but, as he continued his travels across the Antipodes, he observed the overwhelming majority, lots.[10]

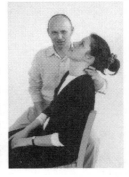

In his own case, F M Alexander had created a technique for putting his important discovery to use. After long and patient study and investigation, he had devised a way of changing the way he directed himself in activity. And as he did so, he got better. But what is even more striking, by the mid eighteen-nineties, he had devised a way a sharing what he had learned with others. At a comparatively young age, he had begun to teach his technique. Significantly, Alexander met with success.

History records that Alexander was so successful at teaching his technique in Australia that, by 1904, at the age 35, he was able to travel to London, to the center of the Empire, armed with letters of recommendation, to bring his work before an even bigger audience. In no time at all, he was teaching his technique to leading actors, business people and physicians. In London society, Alexander was fast becoming something of a star.

In the event, Alexander would continue to teach in London for more than fifty years. He would teach thousands upon thousands of people; he would train others to teach his work; he would write books; he would develop a way of using his hands to communicate his ideas; he would travel to teach abroad. He would continue devoting his life to the teaching of his technique right up until he died in 1955.

© The Society of Teachers of the Alexander Technique.

F M Alexander: The Person

What kind of person was F M Alexander? What about him do we really know?

The first thing to say is that he died before I was born, and I do not believe I have met anyone who knew him firsthand. Yet I, like everyone else interested in this remarkable chap, have built up my own picture. It comes from many places: from reading and studying his articles and books; from all the various written and verbal accounts of people who were trained by him or whose teachers were; from photographs; even from a silent film I have seen. And yet, if I am honest, my picture is hazy. I can't pretend to have a firm grasp of the man.

Most people say he was extroverted, but not all. Most people speak of a wonderful sense of humour, but not all. One person tells us he always had his nose in a book, another that he hardly read at all. Personally, I like to think of him as something of a swashbuckling ladies man, with an impeccable sense of honour, but with sufficient humility never to forget to laugh at himself. Whatever F M was, he was truly remarkable, not least because of the extraordinary impact he made on those whose paths he crossed. Among his more famous pupils were the actors Henry Irving and Lilly Langtree, the American philosopher, John Dewey, the post-War Chancellor of the Exchequer, Sir Stafford Cripps, the then Archbishop of Canterbury, and the writers Aldous Huxley and George Bernard Shaw. We know that he taught and socialized with leading lights in the Sciences, Medicine, The Arts, Politics and Business. We know that many, many thousands of people came to him for help.

But as for F M himself, I am not sure how much I really know; nor, this late in the day, how much I ever really will. There is one thing, however, of which I am reasonably certain in the legacy of F M Alexander, and that is something my teacher, Don Weed, has stressed over and over again, and that is what he wrote and published in his books.

The Books

Over a period of forty years, Alexander wrote and published four books, roughly one a decade. In them, I believe, he gives us as clear a statement of his theory and practice – his technique, as he calls it - as we could wish for. It is largely on the basis of my assisted study of his writings that I present these principles for improvement. There is virtually nothing in this book that is not inspired by ideas Alexander wrote down. And for unlocking their mysteries to me, I must thank again my primary teacher in this field, Don Weed.[11]

The books Alexander wrote are as follows[12]:

Man's Supreme Inheritance (1910, 1918).
Constructive Conscious Control of the Individual (1923).
The Use of the Self (1932).
The Universal Constant in Living (1941.)

The first of these books, *Man's Supreme Inheritance*, was written almost one hundred years ago, so it is helpful to remember that they speak to us from an earlier time. Much water, as we say, has passed under the bridge; many of our paradigms and values have changed. For example, we no longer think the same thoughts about evolution and physiology; and when we use certain words, like "conscious" and "subconscious," we may no longer mean the same thing. These provisos notwithstanding, the ideas in this and his other books, if we take the trouble to read them as he wrote them, are vital and clear. The description of his technique and how to learn it has in fact been written down. In my view, it has been written down well.[13]

Alexander's Principles

In each of his books, Alexander refers over and over again to his principles. He writes about the 'test of principle' and 'working to principle'; he outlines 'the one great principle upon which man's satisfacory progress in civilization depends.'[14] For Alexander, principle is a dominant – if not the most dominant – idea.

These principles, he claims, were arrived at over a long period of investigation and study. His principles form the bed-rock of his technique. He tells us that it is from his principles that all his practices stem.

These days we hear a lot about principles. Many new books are titled, "The Principles of..." We can easily fill in the blanks:

for example, 'yoga,' 'DIY,' 'vegetarian cookery,' or even, 'the Alexander Technique.'

So what is a principle? In the context of Alexander's technique, what does the word *principle* mean?

If we go to the dictionary, we will find many different meanings for the word, ranging from *scruple* to *universal law*. But, in this business of getting better, when we set about learning Alexander's technique, what does principle mean?

Well, to get us started, let me say this: we are primarily (but not exclusively) interested in the idea of principle as a rule for action. We have no need to exclude other meanings, but the meaning we are most interested in is that of *rule*, in the sense of *rule of thumb*, which is just another way of saying *guideline*, or, as I sometimes like to call it, *guiding idea*.

In my *Principles for Improving Your Life* course, I teach principles primarily as ideas or sets of ideas that can be applied to the performance of any or every task. To that extent, I am comfortable thinking of principles as guiding ideas.

"We are primarily (but not exclusively) interested in the idea of principle as a rule for action."

To explain this, I sometimes give the following examples:

'Measure twice, cut once!' is a principle of carpentry, just as, 'Don't criticize, condemn or complain!' is a principle for winning friends and influencing people.[15]

In life, we do not have to measure twice, just as we are free to criticize, condemn and complain. However, experience and reflection have taught at least a few people that, when we ignore these basic principles, we frequently run into problems making tables and chairs, just as we find it difficult to make and keep friends.*

So, without any more ado, here then are my principles for improvement. They are derived from the teachings of F M Alexander. If you take the trouble to consciously and consistently apply them, I feel assured I can guarantee you will improve your life.

*   In chapter 10 I offer a more detailed discussion of principles, with particular emphasis on what it means to work to principle in the living of a life.

Notes

1. From *Notes of Instruction* in *The Alexander Technique* edited by Ed Maisel.

2. The principal sources for the information contained in this chapter are Alexander's autobiographical accounts in *Articles and Lectures* and Chapter 1 of *The Use of the Self*, *Freedom to Change* by F P Jones, *F M Alexander - The Man and his Work* by Lulie Westfeld, *Explaining the Alexander Technique* by Walter Carrington in conversation with Sean Carey, *The Philosopher's Stone - diaries of lessons with F Matthias Alexander* edited by J. O. Fischer.

3. pg 8, *Man's Supreme Inheritance*.

4. pg 35, *What You Think Is What You Get* by Dr Donald L Weed.

5. See page 79, *Man's Supreme Inheritance*, where Alexander writes: "in the human being the neck is very often the indicator of false and inadequate controls."

6. "I found that in practice this use of the parts, beginning with the use of the head in relation to the neck, constituted a primary control of the mechanisms as a *whole,* involving control *in process* right through the organsim, and that when I interfered with the employment of the primary control of my use, this was always associated with a lowering of the standard of my general functioning. This brought me to realise that I had found a way by which we can judge whether the influence of our manner of use is affecting our general functioning adversely or otherwise, the criterion being whether or not this manner of use is interfering with the correct employment of the primary control." pg 10, *The Universal Constant In Living*, Dutton, 1941.

In practice, as the student diminishes the amount of self-generated distortion in this primary relationship, the teacher encounters increased flexibility. This, in turn, is associated with an improvmement in the student's general standard of co-ordination in all activities.

7. pg 42, *The Use of the Self*, the phrase is attributed to John Dewey.

8. pg 61, *Freedom to Change* by Frank Pierce Jones.

9. "Either your head will move in such a way to increase the amount of tension in your neck, to distort all succeeding relationships within you (which will pull you out of shape), and to lower the general standard level of co-ordination of motor activities, or your head will move in such a way that there will be a reduction in muscular overtension, your system will subtly shift to conform to more natural and attractive internal relationships and your motor coordination in the performance of activites will be enhanced." pg 43, *What You Think Is What You Get* by Dr Donald L Weed, DC.

In addition, readers are refered to *Freedom to Change* by Frank Pierce Jones where a number of research papers are cited.

10. A question F M Alexander was often asked by his students in connection with his work is this:

"Why should the use of ourselves go wrong?" [pg 46, *Constructive*

Conscious Control of the Individual.]

Alexander liked to answer, "If you'll tell me why it shouldn't, I'll tell you why it should."

It's the kind of answer that stops most people in their tracks, and for that reason it's very useful when giving an introductory talk, especially if you want to get on to the next thing.

Likewise, if someone asks me these days why we interfere with the poise of the head in relation to the body, I will often reply:

"We interfere because we can. Interfering simply signifies our freedom to choose."

Perhaps, not surprisingly, few students venture a further *why*.

However, we have a little more time here, so I can set out a slightly more detailed answer, based on Alexander's observations about the significance of our living in a rapidly changing world.

In physics, the rate of change of speed is called *acceleration*. And these days, just about everyone would agree that we are living in an accelerating world. The rate of change of just about everything is speeding up. Whether it is in our life-styles, our diets, our relationships, the way products are bought and sold, advertising strategies, business practices, the amount of travel we do, the environment, the way new wars are waged, information technology, the influence of the media, even our shape and size. This trend (and it's importance to human beings) had become apparent to Alexander early on in the course of his investigations. It was a trend that he believed had begun with the emergence of towns and cities.

Fortunately, human beings are extremely adaptable. What is more, we have a remarkable capacity in early life to develop an automatic proficiency in acts we routinely perform. Consider for a moment how quickly children familiarize themselves with computer mouses, and the ease with which most of them cruise the internet after only a small amount of instruction and practice. Consider the fact that most young people learn to ride a bicycle, or write with a pen, and don't forget the skills they have learned. Consider how quickly a child can learn a new language. These things are everyday accomplishments. They are well within almost every child's grasp. Except in cases of serious injury or disease, just about every child starts out with remarkable powers for learning new skills and recalling them with astonishing accuracy.

In later life, the method which the overwhelming majority of people employ to learn new things is to make use of their ability to recall previously mastered proficiencies. If someone wants to learn a new skill, whether it is snow-boarding, speaking Spanish, sending text messages or cooking vegetarian food, they simply call upon the various automatic proficiencies they have already acquired. So that, if the task requires manipulating a stick-like implement, they call upon manual skills previously mastered; if the task requires following written instructions, they recall skills mastered in the class-room long ago; they rely on the accuracy of their automatic recall to get the new job done. And most of the time, this approach works. Most of the time, most people have success with this approach. At least for a while.

F M Alexander recognised, however, that relying on this ability alone represented a great danger to us, for he had seen in his own case, and also that of the countless other people he observed, that his ability to recall past proficiencies accurately was diminishing. He had begun to interfere with the right working of himself, and his general standard of co-ordination had dete-riorated as a result. He had clear evidence of this in his attempts at reciting on stage.

The question that so troubles a great many students is *why*? Why had Alexander's direction of himself in activity gone wrong? Why did Alexander observe similar wrong uses in others everywhere he looked?

After an extensive period of study and reflection, Alexander concluded that it was our collective failure to effectively adapt ourselves to an accelerat-ing world that lay behind the defects he had detected. In our attempts to cope with the demands of a changing world, we were systematically dis-co-ordi-nating ourselves. Modern people were literally buckling under the strain of continuous change.

Alexander believed that in human societies this process of on-going change would never cease. As a consequence, he saw a need for a technique that would help us to acquire an improving flexibility in thought and action, and not be the victim of a deteriorating standard of co-ordination, based upon the automatic recall of past proficiencies. In the absence of such a technique, Alexander believed we were increasingly making ourselves ill, both physical-ly and mentally.

And as every year passes, Alexander's vision becomes ever more apt. For our world is now changing so fast that it demands of us - whether as parents, teachers, workers, artists, business people or even as children - that we keep coming up with fresh responses just to keep pace. It is a world that some-times quite cruelly says to us: "If you don't change with me, you'll perish!" It is a world where, for an ever-increasing number of people, stereotyped or mechanical responses that worked well in the past have less and less value with each passing year. Indeed, if we want to do well in our modern world, we must master a much more general technique: namely, how to come up with an effective response to a quickly changing set of circumstances. We need a technique that generates flexibility in thought and action, that allows us to make on-going changes in ourselves. And it is just such a technique that Alexander created. For Alexander's technique helps us to discover in our-selves that flexibility necessary to thrive in changing times. In this way, if no other, F M Alexander signaled a new direction in a changing world. In this way, F M Alexander was a visionary ahead of his time.

11. For the record, I would also like to mention Majorie Barstow and Frank Pierce Jones, whom Don Weed consistently identifies as his primary teachers.

Marjorie Barstow of Lincoln, Nebraska was the first teacher to be formally trained by F M Alexander, and F P Jones was trained both by F M and his brother, A R.

12. Please refer to the bibiliography.

13. If you should happen to pick up one of F M's books and begin to read, do not be surprised if, on your first reading, you do not understand it all. They are books that require study to understand, in large part because F M is talking about something new. Therefore, attempting to make sense of what is written down in terms of your existing frame of reference will only present obstacles to seeing what is actually written on the page. I myself found that the only way for me to begin to grasp of what F M was actually saying – as opposed to what I assumed he *had* to be saying – was to write each of his books out long-hand 'line-by-line'. I am not advocating you do the same yourself, but I am saying, it worked for me. Personally, even though I had plenty of experience of studying texts, I found his books a challenge to read. You may not, but do not trouble yourself unduly if first time round you do.

14. pg 63, *Constructive Conscious Control of the Individual.*

15. *How to Win Friends and Influencing People* by Dale Carnegie.

Setting Sail

*"Human beings are more alike than unalike,
and what is true anywhere is true everywhere,
yet I encourage travel to as many destinations as possible
for the sake of education as well as pleasure."*

Maya Angelou

One

Psycho-Physical Unity

going to work on the cause

"The body expresses what the mind dwells upon."
Patricia Bollag

Many years ago, my Dad worked as a milk-man, and during the school-holidays I would get up early in the mornings to help him deliver milk. It was fine work in Summer, not so nice in Winter. My Dad, like all the other milk-men, drove a battery-powered milk-float, which must have had a top speed of 25 miles an hour (40 kps for my German friends). One day, we were hurrying along in the float as fast as we could, for some reason eager to get home early. I remember standing next to him in the cab, a bottle of silver-top in each hand, ready to jump out as quick as a flash and make another delivery. But on this occasion something went wrong. He swerved or braked or something, because the next thing I knew I was flying through the air, bottles in hands, heading towards the road.

My first impulse was to stick my hands out in front of me, in a desperate attempt to protect my body and head from the impact with the asphalt. But I couldn't do that as I had glass bottles in my hands; I figured I would slice myself to bits. And so, suspended in mid-air for what seemed like an age, I reasoned out a strategy, a way of protecting myself from the glass.

I folded my arms in front of me, and placed each bottle under the opposing arm. Then I tucked my head and legs in towards me, as best I could turning myself into a ball. I tipped myself forward, endeavouring to make contact with the ground with my shoulder. And then, when I hit, I rolled. I just rolled and rolled. Before I knew it, I was standing on my feet again, staring at the unbroken bottles in my hands. I wasn't cut; I wasn't bruised. My Dad stopped to check I was all right, and I was. We got straight back to delivering milk, with me marveling at my lucky escape.

I have told this story to a number of students, usually as a way of beginning to address the idea that our standard of performance is not fixed, but crucially, as this story illustrates, our standard of performance can change. Our standard of performance can improve; our standard of performance can get worse. To my surprise, many students have countered with stories of their own, of occasions when they exceeded all their expectations and pulled off something remarkable. Often they will report the same experience of time appearing to slow down. One student told me of how he averted a near fatal car crash by a remarkable bit of reasoning and seemingly lightning quick reactions. And yet, as he pulled it off, it seemed to him that he had all the time in the world.

"Every physical creation is preceded by a mental creation."

Stephen Covey

People who excel in sports will often describe a similar experience, characterized by time appearing to slow down, and their enjoying a remarkable degree of co-ordination. They call it, "being in the zone."

Sometimes, however, we hear stories when the reverse happens, when a person suddenly finds themselves incapable of succeeding at a task which routinely they perform well. Except for when it's truly tragic, these events provide great scope for comedy. Think of the young man who is normally a confident and effective speaker, suddenly rendered incapable of stringing two words together when watched by a woman he entertains hopes of attracting. It is all too easy for me to recall times when I have, as we say, "lost it." My first attempts at reading aloud short stories I had penned myself were awful. In response to my anxiety, I was literally a performing disaster. My mind went blank. My voice became weak and faltering. I failed to communicate the sense of the piece, having lost all sense of what the piece was about the moment I laid eyes on my audience. The skills I had honed elsewhere deserted me. At any rate, that's how it seemed. The way I see it now, none of these things happened to me: I did them all to myself.

It is my contention that, in situations like these, when we perform at a higher standard or at a lower one, we do so by changing something about ourselves. The change doesn't just happen; we make the change in our standard of performance happen. We drive our standard up; we drive it down. Or, as most people most often do, they keep it much the same. The responsibility for our standard of performance is ours. It is a mistake to think the cause lies somewhere else. And if you were to ask me how, that is, by what process do we bring the change about, I would have to answer that we change our *thinking*. We start to send out messages to act in a different way.

When I fell out of the milk-float, when I first got up on stage, the change in my standard of performance happened so quickly, it was as if it just changed itself without my intervening. But, when I analyze what actually happened, an explanation in which I play no part just doesn't make sense. An explanation in which the person creating the performance has no active role to play cannot be reconciled to the facts of our experience. Worse, if such an explanation were true, I would have little hope of getting better on the basis of my efforts to change the way I directed myself in activity. I would be incapable of using my ideas to improve my general standard of performance in everything I do. It would mean a great deal of what I am asking you to consider is based on a false premise. So, let's stop a while consider this issue some more.

"Thinking may not be what you think it is."

Martin Cox

In John Gil's first class, I was told that the Alexander Technique was the study of thinking in relation to movement. And what I am saying is this: if and when you study this relationship, if you consider it in the light of experience and common sense, you will discover that it is causal; that is, there is a causal relationship between thinking and movement in which *thinking* is the ultimate cause. Not necessarily in the way that you imagine, because thinking may not be what you think it is[1], but nonetheless, it is thinking, and not the movement of the stars, that causes each and every one of us to move. If we analyze our actions back to their root cause, we always come back to *thinking*, to things I consider to be contained by the broad label *thinking*. And, as Alexander discovered, our thinking is something we can change.[2]

"What you think is what you get."

Don Weed

In class, one way I present the idea that there is a causal relationship between ideas and action is to talk about the neuro-physiology of movement. I tell my students that it is all but universally agreed that humans perform movements by the contraction and relaxation of muscles. And there is just about the same level of agreement that when we do it is messages from the brain via the nervous system that cause our muscles to contract.[3] So the question becomes, what causes the brain to send out the messages that cause us to move? The answer I give to that question is simple: we do. We generate the sending of these messages, and the process we employ to send these kinds of messages is something I call *thinking*. In this sense, everything you do is causally determined by your thinking. Thinking causes movement. Or, as Don Weed likes to say, "What you think is what you get."[4] So, if there is something in your performance you want to improve, then you need to change your thinking. There is no other way. In practice, as F M Alexander discovered, this means going to work on your ideas.

"The design of a movement is a thought."

Don Weed

When I present these ideas in class, most people, though not all, agree. "Sure," they say. "Makes sense to me." So why labour the point? Because, when I watch students perform tasks, whether walking, writing, public speaking or even playing the cello, and I ask them about their attempts to get better, they say things that suggest they believe something very different. When they explain success or failure, they will often do so in terms of things happening outside of themselves, often things over which they have no control. The cause of success, they will tell me, was the teacher's help, the support of the group, or just plain luck. The cause of failure was being watched by others, being put on the spot by the teacher, or a critical word from their spouse. Their standard of performance, they will often tell me, is caused by things over which they have no control. And I have to tell them: no, the cause lies within you; the standard of your performance is driven by what and how you think. If you want to get better, you've got to work on your ideas.

To amplify this point, I frequently ask students to make a distinction in their minds between *reasons* and *causes*. To help them do this, I tell them the following story.

Once upon a time, in a faraway fantasy land, the president of a large and prosperous country summoned his secretary to his office.

The president told his secretary that he needed to make an immediate trip to China, as he wanted to discuss a matter of grave international importance with the Chinese Head of State. The secretary duly began to make arrangements.

A few minutes later, the president's wife came along. "I'm not sure about a trip to China," she said. "Don't you think we should consult the astrologer?"

The president stopped for a moment to consider, then agreed. He told his secretary to stop making arrangements and to summon the astrologer.

The astrologer was told of the president's quandary. He went away to consult the stars and his charts. A few hours later he returned. "There are," he declared, "bad omens regarding a trip away from home in the imminent future. It would be better to postpone the trip."

The astrologer was sent away.

The president then discussed the reading with his wife and concluded that now was a bad time to go to China. So he summoned his secretary and told him to cancel the trip.

That evening, the secretary was discussing the cancelled trip to China with one of the president's advisers. "That damn astrologer," he declared, "has caused the president to cancel yet another important trip."

The astrologer *caused* the president to cancel the trip. But did he? I don't think so. The astrologer simply gave the president reasons for cancelling the trip. To my mind, the president cancelled the trip all by himself. He may have received what he considered to be compelling reasons for cancelling the trip, but it is a mistake to think of the astrologer as the cause. The astrologer merely provided a reason; the president was the ultimate cause.

In class, people often mistake reasons for causes. For example, I hear people say, "The pain in my neck caused me to tighten the muscles in my neck"; or, "The teacher putting their hands on my shoulders caused me to stop holding them up"; or, "My boss shouting at me caused me to go stiff and I've been like it ever since." However, it is more accurate (and ultimately more empowering) to say that in each of these scenarios the student had *reasons* for responding as they did. Often, the reasons were overwhelming. However, the students caused their reactions themselves.

Long ago, I was in a workshop at a conference on group relations when someone said something that left me feeling truly enraged. I was so angry I could barely speak.

Over lunch, I tracked the offending person down, determined to give him a piece of my mind.

"You made me so angry!" I began.

"No, I didn't make you angry," he replied.

"Oh yes you did! I was furious with what what you said."

"No," he said. "You've got it wrong. You made yourself

angry."

"How can you say that? *You* made me so angry! And you're doing it now! Stop it!"

"You're making yourself angry," he said, and walked away.

Alas, he was right.*

I see now that I was the ultimate cause of my reaction. By changing something in myself, I could have reacted in a different way.

We live in a time when it is customary to explain what we do and how we do it in terms of things over which we have no control. People believe that the ultimate cause of success or failure lies in things over which they can exert no influence, for example, their up-bringing, or their environment, or their social class, or the colour of their skin, or their genes. "That boy was born talented," we hear. Or, "With a Mom like that, she never had a chance."

"The true power to change lies in the human will, in the choosing one set of ideas over another."

However, I am putting forward the idea that all these things are influences only: they are not causes. They give us reasons to act as we do, sometimes so compelling it is not easy to imagine how anyone could act any differently. Except, sometimes, people do. Sometimes people confound the world's expectations by choosing against the flow of prevailing ideas.

In this connection, I would like to recommend some books that demonstrate where the true power to change lies: namely, in the human will, in the choosing one set of ideas over anoth-

---

* However, he was giving me *reasons* to be angry. And as I was then, the reasons were truly compelling. I couldn't see how I could react in any other way.

I mention this because some people take the idea of locating the cause of other people's reactions in their thinking so far that they believe they have no responsibility for the reasons they give other people to behave as they do. However, we often give people such compelling reasons to react in certain ways, it is not reasonable to expect them to react otherwise. Knowing this does not alter the fact that the cause of a person's reaction lies in their thinking, but it does impact on how we deal with others and ourselves.

er. Firstly: the autobiography of Maya Angelou, which commences with the volume, "I know why the caged bird sings." Second, "Help Yourself" by Dave Pelzer, and third, "Man's Search for Meaning" by Victor Frankl. In each of these books – and there are many more – we see people choosing against the reasons they were given to act in a given way. People can and do overcome child abuse, torture, racism, a lack of love and education, extreme conditions which we imagine would send almost anyone over the edge. And in each and every case, what marked these people as different, is that they chose to reject the reasons they were given for reacting in a particular way. For whatever reason, these people recognised the power they had to choose their own ideas; they saw that the true power to change lay deep inside themselves.

"But how does this relate to F M Alexander, to his technique for putting ideas into practice, to his vision of bringing about improvements in everything we do?"

Well, at the beginning of his investigation, when F M was suffering from bouts of hoarseness, when he watching himself recite before the mirror, he assumed his problem was physical. Consequently, he searched for a physical diagnosis. Remarkably enough, he found one. He observed that he was pulling his head back down, which was associated with a tendency to depress his larynx and gasp in air, which in turn was associated with a condition of undue muscular tension throughout his body.

Having made a physical diagnosis, Alexander reasoned out a physical remedy. In future, he would adopt the best possible physical conditions for reciting, which would involve preventing those movement behaviours he identified as being associated with his habitual (mis)use of himself. F M attempted to do this by doing whatever *felt natural*. But to his dismay, doing what felt natural did not alleviate his problem. In fact, doing what felt natural was part and parcel of his problem, insofar as doing whatever felt natural was associated with his habitual misuse of himself.

Alexander had come to an impasse. He realised that going to work as he always done would never bring about the improvements he sought. As a consequence, Alexander's investigation took a new and startling turn, for he was forced to consider the question of how he directed himself in activity, that is, by what process or processes did he get himself to recite. What had begun as a purely physical investigation now became a *psychophysical* investigation. He tells us:

> "When I began my investigation, I, in common with most people, conceived of 'body' and 'mind' as separate parts of the same organism, and consequently believed that human ills, difficulties and shortcomings could be classified as either 'mental' or 'physical' and dealt with on specifically 'mental' or 'physical' lines. My practical experiences, however, led me to abandon this point of view and readers of my books will be aware that the technique described in them is based on the opposite conception, namely, that it is *impossible* to separate 'mental' and 'physical' processes in any form of human activity."[5]

"...readers of my books will be aware that the technique described in them is based on the opposite conception, namely, that it is impossible to separate 'mental' and 'physical' processes in any form of human activity."

FM Alexander

After a long and exhaustive study, Alexander concluded that the cause of his unwanted reaction was not in the stars, or his faulty vocal chords, or that he had been taught badly; rather, the cause lay much closer to home: the cause was in himself. As he quotes Shakespeare: "The fault, dear Brutus, lies not in the stars, but in ourselves."

Alexander came to the extraordinary conclusion that the performance of every task - whether reading a book or playing piano, whether composing music or reciting on stage - involved the co-ordinated, inter-dependent working of both 'mental' and 'physical' processes, in which *thinking* plays the causal role. For this reason, if there is something about our performance we

Many people believe that a dulling of the mind, stiffness at the joints, severe physical discomfort and a loss of height are a necessary consequence of getting older. However, what we almost always find is that these effects tend to diminish as students change the way they direct themselves in activity.

wish to improve, for example, the poise of the head in relation with the body, we must go to work on our ideas, specifically our guiding ideas. We must go to work on the *thinking* that generates our unwanted response.

In his own case, F M concluded that his unwanted reaction was brought about by directing himself in activity in an automatic, "unthinking" way. He concluded that he was habitually sending out messages to interfere with the correct use of his musculature, which was associated with a lowering of his general standard of performance in everything he did. To improve, he needed to change the way he directed himself in activity. He would be misdirecting his efforts if worked only on the unwanted response. Instead, he would have to go to work on the cause.

Having thus changed the focus of his investigation, F M Alexander was now aligning his ship the right way.

*

"The fault, dear Brutus, lies not in the stars, but in ourselves."

William Shakespeare

In class, I am frequently called upon to demonstrate the causal relationship between ideas and action in the performance of a given task. As a fairly typical example, one of my students, Lena, a student at the University, recently asked to work on answering questions following presenting a paper in a seminar. In the event, she talked for a few minutes on her specialist subject, then the rest of my group quizzed her avidly. After a couple of minutes, I stopped her and asked her how she was doing.

Not so well, she told me. Lena complained her words were coming out all wrong, and that she was starting to ache in her neck and shoulders. This always happened, she said, when she felt put on the spot in this way.

Significantly, what I had noticed during Lena's performance was the same pattern of muscular interference I had observed when I worked with her on going from sitting to standing. Each time Lena *got ready* to answer a question, she would drive her head back and down, and raise her shoulders and pull them forward. (This same pattern was present all the time, but was amplified in this activity.)

"What are you doing to answer the questions?" I asked.

"Well, I have to lay down tracks in my mind and keep my attention fixed within them. Otherwise, I find I have too many ideas at once which is distracting. Unfortunately, when I think in this way for too long, I get pains in my neck and back."

Significantly, as Lena laid down tracks in her mind, she simultaneously laid down tracks in her body. The thinking she labeled "laying down tracks" was associated with an increase in her habitual misdirection, clearly observable to me, and sensed by Lena as pain.

"Why not experiment answering the questions without laying down tracks?" I suggested.

"But I can't."

"Why ever not?"

"Because I have to when I'm put on the spot. It's the only way I can keep my mind on what I want to say."

"As Lena laid down tracks in her mind, she simultaneously laid down tracks in her body."

So convinced was Lena of this, that I had to place my hands on her in such a way that she was given some fairly persausive reasons for not generating her habitual misdirection.[6] I then got someone to ask her a question, and she found to her surprise that she could easily answer it without laying down the tracks. When she succeeded in this, there was no increase in her habitual misdirection, and consequently she performed at a higher standard and without the pain. For Lena, this was a clear demonstration that it was her manner of thinking that was generating her unwanted response. She realised that if she wanted to get through the next seminar without her usual aches and pains, she had to go to work on her ideas. And in her case, one of the most significant ideas she needed to change was that she could improve her performance by doing what she called laying down tracks. In recognising this, Lena had made tremendous progress.

Many students initially struggle to perceive the relationship between ideas and action in themselves, for the simple reason that they have never before considered the possibility that the cause of their unwanted response lies in their thinking. They have never before considered the guiding ideas that generate both what they do and how they do it. However, for Lena, and for all my other students, there comes a time when they realize that the true source of power, insofar as their general standard of performance is concerned, lies in their ideas.

"But what ideas are you talking about? Which ideas do you mean?"

As I said before, your guiding ideas. Those ideas associated with rules governing both what you do and how you do it.

"But what counts as an idea here? Do you mean the thoughts we think, or do you mean something else?"

In Alexander's work, the word *idea*, just like thinking, has many meanings; in particular, we use the word *idea* to mean *thought*, in the sense of an *idea in mind* or *thought process*, but we also use it to mean *concept*, *belief* or *paradigm*. To that extent, when I refer to guiding ideas, it is important to remember that I may have any or all of these different meanings in mind. For example, Lena employs certain guiding ideas to answer questions which she labels *laying down tracks*, but she also has a conviction concerning the value of *laying down tracks*. This conviction is itself an example of a guiding idea. In practice, she can work to change the guiding ideas she employs to answer questions by, for example, refusing to lay down tracks, or she can seek to undermine her conviction in the value of laying down tracks.

"The body expresses what the mind dwells upon"

Patricia Bollag

We can all work to change the thoughts we think and the way that we think them, but we can also work to change our beliefs, concepts and paradigms associated with the way we direct ourselves in activity.* Indeed, as you make progress on this journey, you will encounter many different ways for changing your guiding ideas, not all of them immediately apparent on first reflection.

But let's return for a moment to Willie, Cynthia and Vicky. If our thinking does in fact cause everything we do and how we do it, then it follows that in each of their cases, improvement will require them to change the thinking that causes their reaction or response. To improve, each of these people will have to go to work on their ideas.

If you remember, Vicky had a good idea she was unable to work to. She had identified a cognitive distortion, but she kept reacting in the same old way. From F M's new perspective, she lacks the necessary guidance and control. Her problem, viewed from this point of view, is a problem of psycho-physical co-ordination. Vicky is unable to act as if her good idea were true. To get better, she has to go to work on her thinking. And as Alexander discovered and I now believe, this means she has to change her ideas.

By the same reasoning, this same principle will apply to Willie and to Cynthia. Improvements for them will necessitate going to work on their thinking, for they must go to work on the cause of their unwanted response. They must go to work on their ideas.

"But which ideas exactly? Can you give examples?"

Certainly. Here are four ideas I frequently encounter.

"Thinking means focusing the attention on a small area and keeping it there."[7]
"We can raise our general standard of co-ordination by exercising specific muscles."

* Please refer to chapter 6 for a more detailed discussion of this point.

"The hip-joint is found on the outside of the leg."[8]

"Our standard of performance is pre-determined by our genes."

Students who are committed to these ideas go to work differently from those who are not. I have also found that students who work to change the way they direct themselves in activity by changing their thinking get different results. Always. For the power to change lies in the students thinking, irrespective of how it seems.

"But if you're right, if my problem is in my ideas, in my thinking, what can I do?"

You can change your thinking.

"I could, I suppose. But I wouldn't know where to begin."

You already have.

"I have?"

Yes. You're already on your way.

"But if I've already begun, then I don't know how to go on."

"There is a causal relationship between the ideas we have and everything we do."

Let me put it like this.

There is a causal relationship between the ideas we have and everything we do. To that extent, if you want to improve, you can help yourself most by changing those ideas that govern both what you do and how you do it. And if you've grasped that, then from my point of view, we've had a really good day. For already, we're sailing our ship the right way.

*

The principle of psycho-physical unity provides us with the necessary leverage to go to work on our thinking if we would make improvements in everything we do. It helps us locate the cause of our reactions in ourselves, and not in events outside.

However, the principle of psycho-physical unity is not a warrant for beating ourselves up, for blaming ourselves for all the mistakes we have made. For if we take the trouble to look closely at our lives, we discover that at each step along the way we had reasons, good or bad, for making the choices we made, for reacting well or poorly. No, we will instead engage ourselves with the task of changing our thinking. If we do this, we can change the way we direct ourselves in the performance of each and every task. If we do this, rest assured, we can improve.

Notes

1. "Thinking may not be what you think it is." - Martin Cox of Bristol.

2. According to Marjory Barlow, F M Alexander's niece and lifetime advocate of his technique, Alexander was fond of saying: "My work is an exercise in finding out what thinking is." [Interview by Frances Oxford in Direction Magazine, Vol. 2, No. 2.]

In addition, Frank Pierce Jones described his initial difficulty in learning the technique as follows: "The big stumbling block for me lay in my concept of thinking." [pg 9, *Freedom to Change*]

To that extent, *thinking* is clearly an important idea.

In my experience, most people bring to the work a far too limited conception of the possibilities contained within this word. Their idea of *thinking* is too limited to engage fully with Alexander's technique. It was true of Frank Jones; it was true of me.

So, let's consider what we might mean by *thinking* here.

In this connection, I once took a course in the philosophy of language at the University of Bristol. One of the things of value I learned was that we cannot discover the meaning of a word like *thinking* by a process of introspection. No, the meaning of any word can never amount to more than the various uses it has in the different regions of language where it is has a role to play. To that extent, we are wasting our time trying to answer questions like: 'What is thinking?' if we attempt to do anything more than the lexicographer (the compiler of the dictionary), who simply lists current and past usage's of the word. It is not possible to study the word and penetrate it's deeper meaning. The word *thinking* only acquires it's meanings from the various ways it is used.

However, we may, when we have reasons to do so, legitimately re-define a word, or restrict or even extend its meaning(s), in order to achieve a particular goal. This happens in Science all the time. Sometimes, the most common meaning of a word is too vague, or too restricted, to get the job done. This being so, when I employ the word *thinking* in the context of Alexander's work, you may fairly ask, "What do I, and teachers like me, mean?"

When I use the word *thinking* in phrases like 'thinking in relation to movement,' or 'thinking in activity,' I am thinking of the largest possible conception of the word. To that extent, *thinking* includes not only thought processes, but attitudes and beliefs as well. In fact, anything that a student might label *thinking* is to be included here, even things many people might not ordinarily label *thinking*, for instance, thoughts about which we are unaware. In my definition, the term *thinking* is very broad.

3. It may be objected that there are a number of involuntary reflexes that do not require the sending of messages all the way from the motor-cortex in the brain in order to initiate movement. However, to the extent that this is a valid objection, for the purposes of the present discussion, I do not consider involuntary reflexes to be movements that are performed. For a fuller discussion of this point, readers are referred to pg 61 of *What You Think Is What You Get*.

4. Please refer to the Bibiliography.

5. pg 21, *The Use of the Self*.

6. How a teacher does this is beyond the scope of this book.

7. see page 9, *Freedom to Change*.

8. The hip joint is in fact located on the inside of the leg.

Two

The Use of Reason

keeping an open mind

"What I intend by the open mind is
the just use and exercize of conscious reason."
F M Alexander

I grew up in the South of England, not far from Hampton Court Palace, once home to Henry VIII. Like many great palaces of its time, it has a maze planted in the gardens. This particular maze comprises a set of hedgerows about eight feet high that form long winding corridors in irregular shapes. The sheer scale and complexity of the design makes for getting to the center, where there is a bench-seat for you to rest, something of challenge. Especially if you're a ten year-old boy. Anyway, I, like most of the adults in there with me, wandered about in this maze for an age, seemingly always coming back to the entrance, but never to the center, which I could glimpse by straining to see through tiny gaps in the hedges. What began as a pleasure was rapidly turning into an ordeal. If it weren't for the fact I had heard people laughing in the middle, I'm sure I would have given up.

And then - and this is important - I stopped to think. Or rather, I stopped what I was doing and started to think. Because all I had been doing up till that point, like most of the people in there with me, was trying to get to the middle as quickly as possible without any so-called thought at all. I, and just about everyone else, had an idea where the middle was, and so we set off in the direction of the middle and then tried one path after another, which before long became the same well-trodden paths, over and over again.

"But what if," I thought for the very first time, "the point of the maze was to get people to trap themselves? Why, then you'd make the most obvious strategy the wrong strategy!" It had to be worth a try. So I walked back to the entrance, and this time all the way back, not just to the start of the short corridor where you could see the entrance, and there, not surprisingly, was a pathway, just where you walked in. It was a pathway I'd no doubt seen but discounted the first time, as it seemed to lead away from the center. I had avoided it. It was too indirect.

It turned out that this pathway skirted round the outside rim for a while, then went straight to the center. I half-expected most people only found it when they gave up trying to solve the problem of the maze and decided to leave. Whatever, I learned a valuable lesson that day. In fact, as I reflect on this story, I learned many. But one of the most important lessons I learned is that people have a tendency to go directly for what they want instead of thinking out the most likely way that they can get what they want. And that is something you can count on. Otherwise the maze wouldn't work. And it is because of this tendency, or habit of thought, as we might call it, that so many of us need Mr Alexander's technique. Because in life we get stuck in many mazes, many of which we have not even realized. And Mr Alexander's technique can teach a way out of life's mazes, because, in its essence, his technique offers a reasoned solution to the problem of getting better in life.

"We can throw away the habits of a life-time in a few minutes if we use our brains."

F M Alexander

As I finish writing that last sentence, it occurs to me that I have just used a word that will ring alarm-bells in some people's heads: that's right, "reasoned." However, in talking about Alexander's work, it's a word we can't avoid. We will come back to it again and again: "reason", or "reasoned", or "reasoning". So, just in case you're one of those people for whom the idea of reasoning is off-putting, just in case you're someone who is now wondering if this technique really is for you, let me tell you another story, this time one of Tennyson's. It was a story F M Alexander liked to tell.

> Having heard that Henry Taylor was ill, Carlyle rushed from London to Sheen with a bottle of medicine, which had done Mrs Carlyle good, without in the least knowing what was ailing Henry Taylor, or for what the medicine was useful.[1]

Poor Carlyle. I'm sure everyone can relate to him. His manner of thinking in this story is familiar to us all. A friend of mine calls it, "acting before you've put your brain into gear." You might call it, "acting on impulse, without thinking, without stopping to consider." There are plenty of adages advising against it, for example, "Look before you leap", or "Think before you act." F M tells us he heard them often enough from his Dad.[2] I heard the same from mine.

F M describes the person behaving in this way as, "being out of communication with their reason." He labels the kind of thinking they employ as "unreasoning."[3]

In F M's day, it stood to reason that there was something problematic, or inferior about, thinking in an unreasoning way. He lived in a time when people celebrated Reason. After all, the Victorians believed that Reason had brought them science and tremendous technological advances. It was the use of Reason that separated humans from animals. It was the great force upon which the advance of civilization depended.

In the twenty-first century, much has changed. Nowadays, reason has a bad press. It has become associated in the popular mind with a mode of thinking (attitude of mind) that is uncreative, rigid, unfeeling. People say, "don't think, feel." It is the advice that Luke Skywalker is given in *Star Wars*. It the advice Anichin is given in *The Phantom Menace*. We are told, "you think too much, you need to get in touch and with your feelings." Everywhere it seems, reason is viewed with a suspicious eye.

However, I am here to tell you that the use of reason, the

"Having heard that Henry Taylor was ill, Carlyle rushed from London to Sheen with a bottle of medicine, which had done Mrs Carlyle good, without in the least knowing what was ailing Henry Taylor, or for what the medicine was useful."

F M Alexander

employment of the reasoning processes, is a foundational idea in Alexander. It is a basic, a fundamental principle. In fact, it is the tool of tools for changing your thinking to raise your general standard of performance in everything you do. It is principle that will most help us to continue our journey well.

Am I crazy? Am I just trying to be controversial? Or could it be that most people have a mistaken, or at the very least contrary, idea about what reason is? These are important questions. And I will answer them, but before I do, I'd like to tell you one more story, this one told by John Paul Getty. It will make what I have to say about reasoning that much easier to follow.

As a young man, John Paul Getty tells us that he threw himself into the oil-business.[4] More or less straight from University, Getty got a crew of drillers together and set about prospecting for oil. These men were tough-minded and independent; they worked long hours at dangerous work, often moving from rig to rig, hoping to strike it rich. Unlike Getty, they had little in the way of a formal education.

One morning, Getty noticed that one of his drillers wasn't working. The man was clearly hungover, and was lounging around on the rig, unwilling or unable to work. The other drillers could see he wasn't pulling his weight.

Getty was the man in charge; it was his rig, and he knew he had to say something, or everyone else in his crew would think they could get away with not working. But a reprimand from a 22 year-old who looked like he'd never been on rig before was, in his view, likely to turn the driller and the rest of the crew against him. Getty was stuck. He didn't what know what to do. But he couldn't do nothing. Something had to be done.

For some reason, when I first heard this story, I could relate to the young John Paul Getty. Maybe because I had been in situations when running training courses, when I was the youngest in the room, when everyone else seemed to have plenty more experience than me on the topic we were exploring, yet it was my job to take the issue forward. Whatever, I identified with

Getty and I felt stumped. 'What does a fellah do?' I thought. I was back in the maze, except I no longer believed there was a pathway to the center.

Well, this is what John Paul Getty did. He went over the hungover driller in full view of the rest of the crew, who immediately pricked up their ears, eager to hear what the new boss had to say. Then Getty confounded everyone's expectations. He bet the driller a day off work with full pay in a race to the top of the rig. On top of that, he said he'd give the hungover driller a ten-second head-start. The whole crew got excited. Gambling on the outcome of a potentially dangerous race was a language everyone understood. The driller agreed to the wager.

In the event, Getty just won the race. He tells us that the driller worked his heart out all day, as he had lost the bet and his honour (paying up on a lost bet) was now at stake. It nearly killed him. The rest of the crew took a shine to Getty. He had made his point in a way that gained their approval. In a race fairly won, no one lost face. Getty tells us that there were never again problems with hungover drillers on that particular rig.

"Reasoning has something to do with thinking things out, with finding solutions to problems, with engaging the conscious mind."

Fantastic! I was mightily impressed. No wonder John Paul Getty became the richest man in the world. But, of much more importance - at least as far as I am concerned - is that Getty reasoned the whole thing out. He considered his situation and he came up with a solution. He didn't act on impulse. He didn't act without thinking. He engaged his conscious mind. To that extent, we may fairly say that he employed his reasoning processes. And that's because reasoning has something to do with thinking things out, with finding solutions to problems, with engaging the conscious mind.

*

In class, when I have introduced the use of reason as a founding principle, when I have said that we will continue our journey by seeking to engage our minds with the task of getting better, some students say, "Sure, great, I like that. Let's move on."

Others, however, are not so happy. For them, the use of reason as a basic principle is problematic. I, myself, when I was first introduced to Alexander's work, was just such a person. In 1995, as far as I was concerned, I needed to do anything but reason to get better. Consequently, I am not troubled now, if, when I first introduce this principle, a number of my students balk. For I am only too well aware that students have good reasons for not wanting to commence the journey here. On the one hand, some students claim that they can't reason, or at least not very well; on the other, some students believe that there is something intrinsically wrong with the use of reason as a founding principle. I myself was in this second camp. As far as I was concerned, I was already reasoning too much. I needed to do anything but reason more.

Before addressing people who were like me, I'd like first to say a few words to the student who says, "I can't reason." In practice, this objection can take many forms: 'I'm not much of a thinker'; 'I could never do science at school'; 'I can't solve problems'; 'I never come up with any original ideas'; 'I'm just not a creative thinker.'

First, let me share with you one of my all-time favourite Alexander stories. As far as I know, it first appears in the Alexander literature in Frank Pierce Jones' book, *Freedom to Change*:

> It is said a simple way to trap a monkey is to present him with a nut in a bottle. The monkey puts his hand through the bottle's narrow mouth, grasps the nut, then cannot withdraw his paw because he will not (and hence cannot) let go of the nut.[5]

One of my students assures me this is actually how it's done. In places where they need to catch monkey's, for example to seek out clean water in a drought, a bottle with a nut in it will often do the trick. This last year, following the example set by my teacher, Don Weed, I have presented the problem of the monkey-trap to students in my classes. I ask them, "If you were the monkey, what would you do to get the nut?"

I have never yet met a student who was unable to come up with a solution to this problem. Each and every student has figured their own solution out. True, some solutions appear better than others, but each and every student has figured their own solution out.

Most students say they would let go of the nut then tip it out. (Not me, however. First time, it simply didn't occur to me that if the nut got in there, it had to come out). Others students opt for more original solutions. One said she'd suck the nut out. Another went for the macho approach: he told me he'd smash the bottle with a log. Yet another told me he'd go and get something else to eat.

People can and do solve the problem of the monkey-trap; they can engage their reasoning minds. When people tell me they can't reason, I tell them: reasoning is something you already do. It is something that living a life in the twenty-first century demands. You use your reasoning processes every time you figure something out, every time you solve a problem that comes your way.

"You use your reasoning processes every time you figure something out, every time you solve a problem that comes your way."

More often than not, the belief that a person can't reason arises because they don't use the label "reasoning" to describe certain kinds of thinking they employ. But reasoning does not have to involve pencil and paper. Reasoning can come in many a varied guise.

In this connection, the famous chemist, Kekulé, spent many years trying to work out the molecular structure of benzene. He thought and researched and thought, but he just could not figure it out. Then one night, so it is claimed, after another seemingly fruitless day's work in his laboratory, he fell asleep and had an amazing dream. In his dream, he met a snake with it's tail in its mouth. Kekule awoke to realize he had solved the problem of benzene. Each molecule was attached to another to form a ring.

Let me assure you: Kekulé reasoned the solution out. He engaged his conscious mind with the problem of the molecular structure of benzene and he came up with a solution. It is true the solution came about in an unexpected way. He wasn't at his desk when he stumbled upon the answer to his question. But he found his solution by engaging his reasoning processes. Kekulé solved the problem of the molecular structure of benzene by engaging his conscious mind.

Sometimes, I have to tell my students that reasoning is not what they always took it to be; reasoning is different to what they had all along imagined. But make no mistake: reasoning is a capacity everyone has. If you are reading this book, then you have the capacity to reason, and to reason well. That means you can plan, you can create, you can problem-solve, you can be original.

"Reasoning is the hallmark of the open mind."

In human beings, the capacity to reason is simply in-built, just like bones and muscles to move them. However, some of us are - how shall I say? - more than a little un-practised in its use. In which case we may need to exercize our powers of reasoning; and that doesn't mean doing logic puzzles, which would be to focus on a tiny, if nonetheless important aspect of reasoning. No, if wish we wish to work to this principle, we will instead engage our minds with the task of getting better.

"And how do you propose I do that?" someone might ask.
Just continue what you are doing now.
"What do you mean?"
Just continue engaging with the ideas I am presenting.
"That will do?"
For now, yes. Just continue engaging with the ideas I am presenting.
"But, but, but...!" I can hear my former self cry out. So, just in case you are like me, before we press on to explore a more

concrete application of this principle to our journey, let me spend a while dealing with the other set of objections to the use of reason as a founding principle. Trust me, some people do object. Even if it's only to go silent in class, or to walk out the door never to return.

Back in 1995, if asked, I would have said: "I want to use my imagination, not my reasoning processes." I wanted to write fiction, but I was finding it increasingly difficult. The way I saw it, I was employing my reasoning processes at work, and *that was* my problem: I continued with this mind-set when I wanted to write. What I needed was to use my imagination. What I needed, I believed, was to stop thinking in an orderly, rational way.

In her highly successful and highly valuable book, *The Artist's Way*, Julia Cameron makes a distinction between what she calls

"What is required is not prejudice in either direction, but a calm, clear, open-eyed intelligence, a ready, adaptive outlook, an outlook, believe me, which does not connote indefiniteness of purpose or uncertainty of initiative."

F M Alexander

artists brain and logic brain. She uses this distinction to encourage blocked artists to abandon certain types of thinking in favour of more creative alternatives. She writes:

"[*Logic brain*] thinks in a neat, linear fashion. As a rule, logic brain perceives the world according to known categories."

By contrast: "*Artist brain* is our inventor, our child, our very own absent-minded professor."[6]

The way I see it now, what Cameron presents here suggests a false dichotomy, for the simple reason that so many people equate logic with reason, and art with imagination. (I know I did.) As a consequence, they are led to make an either/or choice. A more helpful distinction, if we choose to make one, is open mind versus rigidity of mind.[7] And, like Alexander, I believe that reasoning is the hallmark of the open mind. So much so that in my world, as in Alexander's, reasoning is associated with the free play of the imagination. An open mind allows for the free play of new ideas.

As Alexander wrote in 1910: "What I intend by the open mind is the just use and exercize of conscious reason."[8]

I have come to see that imagining and reasoning are not opposites, but interlocking pairs. They are like hills and valleys, or heads and bodies.

I have come to see that imagining and reasoning are not opposites, but interlocking pairs. They are like hills and valleys, or heads and bodies. The true enemy of creativity is not logic, nor is it order, but rigidity in thinking. The enemy of Art is a mind that wants no truck with anything new. For if we use our reasoning processes to solve the monkey-trap, if it was his reasoning processes that John Paul Getty employed to find a solution to the problem of his hungover driller, then the use of reason involves more than simply deduction, or making a logical connection between ideas: reason is associated with creativity, with the working out of new ideas.

By 1995, I had got myself into an either/or mind-set. I believed I was able either to think things through or engage my imagination. I was living that opposition, that false dichotomy. I had come to believe that the kind of thinking I employed to train adults was somehow antithetical to the kind of thinking I

needed if I was to write. As a consequence I could only do one
or the other. As this dichotomy grew, so it seemed I was forced
to make a choice between work and writing fiction. I was
increasingly unable to bridge the gap in myself. As time passed
by, I was tearing myself further apart.

Happily, I no longer see it that way. The manner of thinking
we adopt to get any job done is always a choice. And we do not
have to limit ourselves in any one direction. We can, if we so
choose, engage the whole of minds in the acts and art of life.

I remember once, when I first introduced the idea of reasoning
to a class, a hitherto eager student suddenly looking downheart-
ed. When I asked her about it, she told me that she had held out
great hope that Alexander's work could help her, but not anymore. She told me that she had been trying to rely on her feelings more, to develop an intuitive approach to life, and because
this approach had helped her so much, she wasn't about to give
it up. "I have learned the value of relying on my gut-feelings,"
she said.

*The true enemy of cre-
ativity is not logic,
nor is it order, but
rigidity in thinking.*

You may be surprised by this – I know she was - but I have
no intention of arguing against intuition, or gut-feeling, or that
little voice inside your head that whispers advice. What I will do,
however, is ask you to consider, in your own case:

What distinguishes a gut-feeling from a prejudice?

Or:

What distinguishes an intuition from an impulse?

These are important questions, and to answer them well we will
need to travel far on the voyage that Alexander made. For
Alexander discovered, just as I have in following him, that the
faculty we call intuition, or gut-feeling, becomes ever-more reliable as we work to the principle of the use of reason in the living of our lives. It is by engaging our minds that we refine them,

that we become open to insights we would otherwise overlook.*

The role of reason in developing intuition is an important topic, and, as the book progresses, I will have a chance to address this issue more fully. I will explain to you how, to my mind, Alexander's work can build our trust in the little voices, whether in writing a book or teaching a class - not by jettisoning the reasoning processes, but by engaging them more fully.

You may remember in *Star Wars* Luke Skywalker is told: "Don't think, feel!"

All I am suggesting is that, instead of abandoning our reasoning processes, we might more profitably construe advice such as this as: "Quit thinking in your mechanical, unreasoning way!"

So let's be clear: I am not rejecting having convictions, or faith, or even trust. Later, I am going to assert that, rightly understood, trust is something we need. But not that trust which cannot be questioned. And that's because asking questions is necessary if we would get better. Asking questions is the beginning of changing ideas. Asking questions is necessary to improve.

At bottom, objections such as mine are based on the idea that the use of reason will somehow limit us. They arise because people consider reasoning in its most restrictive sense; that is, they impose a restriction. But remember me in the maze, or falling from the milk-float, or John Paul Getty on the rig. As far as I am concerned, the thinking we employed is best described as reasoning. It relates to creativity in thinking, to finding solutions to problems, to thinking in new and unexpected ways. To use reason is to engage the conscious mind. It is not to place

---

*   It occurs to me that a tough fact to face for those who argue against reasoning in favour of "intuition" is that our gut-feelings do occasionally mislead us. Our so-called intuitions are in fact sometimes wrong. In my observation, this happens most often when our reaction is motivated by uncomfortable feelings, such as shame, guilt, or fear. Whereas, so far as I have been able to discern, our intuition is far more reliable when we are able to engage freely with an open-minded assessment of the facts

limits on the mind. For me, as for Alexander, reasoning and open-mindedness are inseparable.

Some people do not believe this. So much so that when they perform the function they label as reasoning they impose limits on themselves. They narrow their minds instead of engaging them; they close their minds down instead of opening them up. But this has nothing to do with reasoning, with what I am calling reasoning. In my world (and in Alexander's), the use of reason is associated with the free play of the imagination. It involves not placing mental restrictions on the bubbling up of new ideas. It involves thinking things through with an open mind.

When a person thinks as they have always done, when they think in fixed and automatic ways throughout the daily round of their life - whether they call what they are doing reasoning or not - they are placing a restriction upon the use of their reasoning processes. They are, at least to some extent, deadening their conscious minds. For as F M Alexander discovered and I now believe, to reason is to undo the limits imposed by our unthinking use of ourselves.

"Okay. But how does the use of reason relate to our journey? What significance does it have for people like Willie, or Vicky, or Cynthia?"

Let's go back to Alexander's story. Early on, if you remember, F M discovered the importance of the relationship of head to neck, and head and neck to torso, insofar as he wanted to bring about improved conditions in reciting. However, his success in applying this discovery was limited. He found it much more difficult than he had at first presumed to put his discovery into practice. All too often he reverted to what he called his habitual use of himself. As a consequence, he was forced to consider the question of the direction of the use of himself. He tells us that this was something that he, like almost all of us, had never thought about before. He got himself to perform in the way that *felt natural* to him. In other words, he directed himself without "thinking." That is, so far as the direction of himself was concerned, he had made no attempt at engaging his conscious mind. It was a strategy that had worked fine in the past, but it was a strategy that wasn't working now. The old way of going to work, of directing himself without conscious thought, of doing what *felt natural*, was now associated with his vocal problems, with what he called his habitual (mis)use of himself.

Alexander was indeed in a hole. The only way he knew of directing himself in activity wasn't working well enough to bring about the improvements he sought. What could he do? Well, like me in the maze, like John Paul on the rig, like Frank Jones' monkey, he could try to figure out a solution to his problem: he could engage his conscious mind. And that's precisely what Alexander did. He engaged his conscious mind. He came up with a solution to his problem. And that solution was as breathtaking as it was original. He would seek to employ his reasoning processes in the direction of himself. Where previously he had relied upon an automatic or habitual direction of himself, he would endeavour to employ a reasoning one. So far as the direction of himself was concerned, Alexander would work to a new principle. He would seek to engage his reasoning mind.

And if, like F M, you want to succeed in putting your good ideas into practice, if you want to enjoy an ever-increasing improvement in yourself in everything you do, then you need to engage your conscious mind. Like F M, you too will have to figure out a solution to the problem of changing the way you direct yourself in activity.

F M's solution, or at least the first step of his solution, was to extend the scope of reason. He would employ his reasoning processes in the direction of himself. Instead of continuing to do what *felt natural*, he would engage his reasoning mind.

F M Alexander writes about reasoning in all his books, and when he does, he contrasts reasoning with fixed habits of thought, that is, of going to work in an habitual, automatic kind

"The centre and backbone of my theory and practice is that THE CONSCIOUS MIND MUST BE QUICKENED."

F M Alexander

of way. You may well decide (even on the basis of a reasoned assessment of the facts) that it is a mistake to seek to employ your reasoning processes in the direction of the self. That we are better off continuing to do whatever *feels natural*. And if you do: great. Because there is nothing wrong with going to work in an automatic, "unthinking" way. In fact, for some people that way of thinking works very well a good deal of the time. My argument is that won't lead to an enjoyment of all of your potentialities; in fact, all my experience as a teacher of Alexander's work suggests it leads to a gradual deterioration in the quality of your performance. Going to work in an unreasoning way has led everyone I have ever taught along a downhill slope. Working to the unreasoning principle leads, as far too many people are only too painfully aware, to the gradual ossification of mind and body, to a gradual deterioration in everything we do.

To that end, if you are minded to follow with me on this journey, let us agree that we will work to the principle of the use of reason as we venture on. The use of reason will provide a foundation to which we can always return; we can and will depend upon reason as a guide. Whenever we don't know, when we are unsure what to think or which way to go, we will make decisions that make sense to us, that appeal to our reasoning minds. In short, we will engage our minds with the task of getting better.

We will keep an open mind.

Notes

1. pg 9, *Man's Supreme Inheritance.*.
2. pg xiv, Preface to *Man's Supreme Inheritance.*.
3. pg 44, for instance, *Man's Supreme Inheritance*
4. pg 78, *How To Be Rich.*
5. *Freedom to change.*
6. pg 12, *The Artist's Way.*
7. Refer to *Habits of Thought and Body* in *Man's Supreme Inheritance.*
8. pg 53, *Man's Supreme Inheritance.*

Three
Prevention
as if we were well-made...

"Like a good fellow, stop the things that are wrong first."
F M Alexander[1]

Everyone has heard the saying, "prevention is better than cure," but few appear to have grasped its practical application in the field of self-improvement.

Significantly, the principle of prevention is central to the teachings of F M Alexander. Prevention is quite simply a dominant idea. And as a teacher of his work it is my job to tell you that if you succeed in working to this principle you will turn your life around. You will live your life with a new and transforming idea. So what is it, this principle of prevention? When Alexander talked about prevention, what exactly did he mean?

"You are perfect as you are, except for what you are doing to yourselves."

F M Alexander

On the 17th October, 1996, my son, Leif, was born. Without doubt, this was one of the most joyous and defining moments of my life. Chloe had been magnificent, and Leif was a miracle beyond words.

Back then, if you remember, I was running a growing training and consultancy business. Prior to Leif's birth, my plan had been to take six weeks paternity leave, so I could be at home with him and Chloe. However, I soon found myself making little trips to the office. It wasn't that much of a problem, until Leif developed a hernia in his groin. He was only three weeks old.

Our doctor assured us that having an inguinal hernia wasn't too serious, and that we should wait six months before having an operation, as surgery on new born babies was risky. In the meantime, his condition was to be monitored.

Two weeks later, I drove to Cheltenham to give a speech to launch my new drugs education book. I had just started speaking when someone passed me an urgent message. That morning, it transpired, Leif had got suddenly worse, so Chloe had taken him to the Children's Hospital in Bristol. Upon examination, a consultant declared that he had developed a blockage in his intestines and that he needed immediate surgery.

I made my apologies and left.

A long and difficult night lay ahead. Forms had to be signed and decisions had to be made.

Happily, the operation was a complete success. However, I didn't go into work for the next few days and so failed to submit a tender and thereby lost an important training contract. It virtually ensured I'd have to make a member of staff redundant. It seemed I was needed in two places at once, and that I couldn't be. I was in turmoil. For the first time in a long while, I didn't know what to do.

By then, you may recall, I had been having Alexander lessons for about a year, and I kept thinking about an aphorism attributed to F M Alexander, "If you stop the wrong thing from happening, the right thing happens by itself."[2]

It was clear that I wanted to spend time with Chloe and Leif. Also, I wanted to write; and I wanted to learn more about Alexander's technique. What if, I asked myself, for now at least, running my business was wrong? What if, so long as the bulk of my life was filled with organising drugs education training, there would never be space for the right thing to appear? With these thoughts racing through my mind, I booked flights for Chloe, Leif and me to visit our friends in California. I was determined to take the rest of my paternity leave.

A couple of weeks later I was in San Francisco. As I carried Leif up and down the hilly streets, it dawned on me that it was time to abandon Gil, at least the drugs education part. But I knew I couldn't. Because then I'd have to make the rest of my staff redundant. And besides, how would we live? But the more I thought about it, the clearer the *wrong* became.

Somehow, once I got back to England with a decision made, a solution appeared. Two members of staff said they'd like to take over the drugs education side of the business. And after some wrangling with the Home Office, a large contract was handed over to them. At the same time, Don Weed announced he was beginning a new Alexander teacher training course in Bristol. Meanwhile, I started writing fiction again. My drugs book sold well and I collected royalties. By a seeming miracle, life went on.

Six years later, Leif is at school and I write, both fiction and non-fiction; also I teach improvement classes inspired by the teachings of F M Alexander. I still run Gil, but we no longer offer drugs education training. As you might expect, I now have a different understanding of Alexander's aphorism. Now, it is tied up with the principle of prevention. It has a specific meaning in the context of how we direct ourselves in activity. However, as an idea that can be applied more generally, I continue to reflect on it in the context of my life as a whole. And I would encourage you to do the same. "If you stop the wrong thing from happening, the right thing happens by itself."[3]

Well-madeness

Thirty years ago, Don Weed introduced the concept of "well-madeness" in his search to find better and better ways of teaching F M Alexander's work. Since graduating as a teacher, I have used this concept to introduce the principle of prevention to my students. I find that it provides me with a simple and effective way in.

In class, I introduce well-madeness using the following chart. It dates back, I believe, to the early seventies, when Don first invented it.[4]

Dr Don's Wellmadeness Chart

Are you **poorly-made** and have to 'do' something to perform *well?*	OR	Are you **well-made** and have to 'do' something to perform *poorly?*

(In the absence of injury or disease.)

Well? What do you think?

The majority of students come to my class believing that they are poorly-made. They are convinced of the need to do something to perform well. I encourage them to consider an alternative idea.

In class, I ask my students to consider the practical application of well-madeness to their lives.

"What would happen," I ask them, "If you designed your actions on the basis of the idea that you were well-made? How would you have to change?"

And then we experiment. We sit, stand, walk, write, draw; we squat, kneel, bend, speak, sing. We see what happens when a person works to stop their unnecessary 'doing', rather than adding corrective movements in. I like the results. Always. From my point of view, the standard of performance always gets better. The experiments deepen my conviction in the idea that we are well-made. So my advice to my students and to you is: "see what happens if you go to work AS IF you were well-made."

When I introduced the concept of well-madeness to a class the other week, one of the students raised a hand to object. "We are not well-made," he said. "We are full of physical imperfections and lack of symmetry. Well-madeness is the exception, not the rule."

Fair points; both. Unfortunately, they arose from a failure on my part to make explicitly clear what I meant. Well-madeness does not mean it is not possible for mistakes in our design to occur. A visit to the local Children's Hospital would quickly lay that mistaken idea to rest. Nor does well-madeness mean that we can't become injured in such a way as to undermine our capacity to perform well: broken bones and head injuries are obvious examples. No, well-madeness says that, "in the absence of injury or disease, we perform as if we were well-made." When we stop sending ourselves wrong, we move in a co-ordinated and mechanically efficient way.*

Well-madeness suggests that, if we stop sending ourselves wrong, we will improve: that is, we will perform at a higher standard. There are many persuasive arguments for why this should be so, but in an introductory book of this kind, they will only be room for me to describe the concept and it's practical application, and to suggest some fruitful lines of inquiry for the eager student.

Most people, however, if we are to judge them according to their deeds, believe that they are not well-made. They spend hours, days, weeks, years, trying out things to do in order to get better, rather than seeking to prevent whatever it is they are doing wrong. The idea of a flaw in their design has taken hold. They are searching for something to do to put themselves right. But what if, I ask them, so far as co-ordination and ease of

---

* Incidently, the degree to which we lack symmetry is often much smaller than most students imagine, for we find that a great deal of our lack of symmetry disappears when we make progress in Alexander's work. In most cases, when we find one shoulder significantly higher than the other, it is because the student keeps it higher by the more or less permanent activation of muscles, or keeps the other lower by the same means.

movement were concerned, the flaw was in the application and not the design? What if we would all perform well, except for when we did something, or thought something, to meddle with ourselves?

In my experience, this a fruitful question to consider. What if, I ask my students, the capacity to fall from a milk-float in a reasoned and co-ordinated manner was part of my design, of everyone's design, if only we knew how to access it?

What if?

F M Alexander was a Victorian. He believed not only in Reason but also in evolution. He believed that in the natural world things had evolved to work well. For him, evidence of some purpose running through life was all around us. In nature, where Alexander spent a good deal of his early life in Tasmania, there was evidence of a plan. To that extent, it is not surprising that he reasoned as follows: if reciting as he did brought about a loss of voice and resting made it better, then there was something about his manner of reciting that constituted a misuse of the parts concerned. His starting point here is that he expects his mechanism to work well unless he sends it wrong. It was this idea that led him to ask the right kind of questions to develop his life's work. At the very beginning, he set about preventing what he was doing wrong. And he had success almost immediately. Once he stopped pulling his head back down he got better. The improvement was as startling as it was immediate. He took a huge step forward by simply working to prevent what he did wrong.

Another huge figure of Alexander's time was Sigmund Freud (1856-1939). He, too, believed in Reason and in evolution. Like Alexander, there is evidence he believed things had evolved to work well.

Freud's life's work began with an observation and a simple piece of reasoning. In Freud's case, what struck his attention were seemingly innocuous slips of the tongue. For Freud, if the words we utter do not come out as we intend them, there is evidence of some interference. Why? Because he expects there to be a correlation between what we intend to say and what we actually say. In the absence of interference, just like Alexander, he expects things to work well.

For me, the parallels in the origins of Freud's work and Alexander's are simply extraordinary. In both cases, they began by investigating the apparent disparity between what they intended and what they actually did in speaking. Alexander noticed he was pulling his head back and down; Freud noticed himself and others make repeated slips of the tongue. Significantly, both men concluded there had to be some kind of interference. Why? Because both men believed things had evolved to work well.

In the event, Freud postulated the existence of an unconscious mind. His life's work became it's on-going investigation. Alexander, on the other hand, concerned himself with an investigation into how he directed himself in activity; he wanted to know what he was doing wrong and how he could, as a first step, prevent it.

Unlike Freud, Alexander had no interest is denying or affirming the existence of an unconscious mind. In his first book, *Man's Supreme Inheritance*, he chose instead to make a distinction between subconscious and conscious thought. He defined subconscious thinking as automatic, habitual, rigid; he associated subconsciousness with fixed habits of thought. Conscious thought, by contrast, was associated with reasoning, with an engaged and open mind.

Alexander knew from his own firsthand experiences in Tasmania that wild animals had evolved to move well. At the same time, he had observed that human beings living in so-called civilized societies frequently developed defects in the way they moved. Committed to a belief in the theory of evolution, Alexander inferred that the problems modern people were experiencing in the direction of themselves represented the movement from one stage of evolution to another: namely, the change from subconscious to conscious guidance and control. As the power of our conscious minds had increased, so we had become more able to interfere with that subconscious guidance that otherwise would work perfectly well. This was not a failure of evolution, this was no evidence that the evolutionary plan was spent; it was instead a pointer to the next stage in our evolutionary growth. Alexander believed that we could continue this process of evolution by learning how to consciously prevent interference in the right working of ourselves. For in the absence of interference, just like Freud, Alexander believed things had evolved to work well.

"It is the recognition in practice of the principle of prevention which makes possible man's advancement to higher and higher stages of evolution and opens up the greatest possibilities for human activities and accomplishment."

F M Alexander[5]

I do not wish to entangle myself in Alexander's evolutionary argument. I have little idea what current thinking on evolution is, or how accurate Alexander's model will one day prove to be. My point here is simply to highlight the principle of prevention and the thinking that supports it; the idea that, as a first step, we are best served if we seek to stop what we are doing wrong as opposed to trying to put things right. For, if it is true we have evolved to work well – for the reasons Alexander cites or for others - that we are born with an innate co-ordination, that our psycho-physical mechanisms have evolved so that we can readily translate our ideas into practice, then it follows that all we need to do to improve is to prevent ourselves from sending ourselves wrong. There will be clear benefit in going to work as if we were well-made.

As FM used to say: "If you stop the wrong thing from happening, the right thing happens by itself."

Many of my students tell me they accept the idea of being perfect as they are *in theory*. However, a significant proportion confess they have trouble putting this idea to work. All too often, when we explore working to this new principle in class, we encounter a deep-seated conviction that they are somehow physically or mentally defective, that they must, accordingly, *do something* to right themselves. And the doing they adopt, more often than not, creates a significant and debilitating interference in the right working of the head in relation to the body, which serves to undermine their general standard of performance in everything they do.

"But if I didn't do *this*," they tell me (referring to some unnecessary muscular activity), "I'd be too tall... too short... too crooked... too fat." Or: "If I stopped doing *that*, I'd be too stupid... clever... too much of a dreamer... too aloof... too strong... too weak."

As a consequence these students create movement behaviours that are associated with a deterioration in the quality of their performance. To improve, I tell them they can help themselves by, as a first step, working to relinquish their debilitating idea.

In this connection, I'd like to report that, at five-feet four inches, I am what at least some Americans would call vertically-challenged: that's 1.63m to my European friends. However, if the occasion demands, I can make myself even shorter by contracting muscles to increase the cervical and lumbar curves in my spine. I demonstrate this movement behaviour in class in such a way that all of my students can see it. But I can also, by the same process of contracting muscles, make myself taller by reducing the cervical and lumbar curves. I will demonstrate this movement in class as well. (Not for too long, as after a short while I start to ache.) To most people, this looks as if I've got a poker shoved up my you-know-where. After a while, most of the students become uncomfortable watching. Most of them prefer me as I was before.

So I stop.

I explain to my students that I can be shorter or taller: for me, it's a simple matter of choice.

Then I ask them to imagine that I was someone who really believed in being taller (or shorter), who really thought I'd look better, or in some concrete way be better, if I gained (or lost) an

"Everyone is teaching one what to do, leaving us still doing the things we shouldn't do."

F M Alexander

At ease

Shortened

Stretched

inch.

"Will you do that?"

They nod.

"If I was such a person, can you imagine that I'd find the energy for the extra work, especially if, after a little while, I ceased to be aware I was making it?"

They nod again.

Then I ask:

"Can you imagine anyone else acting like that? Can you imagine anyone else creating a more or less permanent distortion in themselves if they thought there was benefit in it?"

They nod their heads to agree.

"Can you imagine the same thinking in yourselves?"

For me, there is nothing intrinsically beautiful about shrivelled, shrunken, stunted, cramped or diminished; just as there is nothing intrinsically beautiful about long-winded, inflated, bloated, stretched, or "on the rack". As a teacher of Alexander's work, my strong preference is for my students and for me to be our own size, whatever that may be. For when we stop trying to turn ourselves into something we are not, not only do we give ourselves a break, but everyone else gets a reprieve. Just about everyone else prefers us without unnecessary movements added in.

*

The idea of *the wonderful potentialities of man*[6], that we are perfect as we are, that we already possess all that we need, is gaining ground.

In his book, *If You Want to be Rich and Happy, Don't Go To School*, Robert Kiyosaki tells of seeing the genius in the eyes of a friend's new-born baby:

... as I held the child in my arms, it looked up at me and smiled. The child's eyes were wide, bright and full of wonder, amazement, excitement and anticipation of this gift called life. The child smiled its toothless smile, drooled and squirmed a little in my arms. Though I was a stranger, the child's eyes expressed love, without fear or reservation. There was communication between two souls. The spark I saw in the child's eyes was the spark of love – and in that moment the genius in both of us met.[7]

This experience, Mr Kiyosaki tell us, was the forerunner of a recognition of the genius in the every newborn child.

Maxwell Maltz tells us of his conviction that we are all born with a success mechanism: we all have the capacity to succeed.[8]

Julia Cameron tells us that creative recovery involves removing blocks we have placed in our way; she believes we are all born with creative potential.[9]

Similarly, anyone who has spent time with young children will tell you that moving well is an everyday accomplishment; the majority of children exemplify a standard of co-ordination in activity which, sadly, the majority of adults lack.

Assuming Kiyosaki, Maltz and Cameron are right, do most of us lose these gifts, these potentialities, these inner and outer freedoms as we get older? Do they pass from us like our first teeth never to return? In my view: no. Emphatically not.

I concur with F M Alexander that we are perfect as we are, except for what we do to ourselves[10]. In the absence of injury or disease, we move as if were well-made. This truth is validated in my teaching day-in and day-out. I see the same principle at work when I watch my own and other teachers teach. There is nothing to do to improve our psycho-physical co-ordination, to recover our capacity to reason and move well. These potentialities are not dead and buried simply because, in recent times, we may have seen evidence of them less.

It has been my consistent experience that the results are

For most young children, moving well is an everyday accomplishment.

nothing short of miraculous when we help students as a first step to stop.

The principles of psycho-physical unity, the use of reason and prevention, in conjunction with Alexander's discovery, provide us with a solid foundation for bringing about on-on-going and lasting improvements in everything we do. For we can employ our reasoning processes to go to work on our thinking to stop sending ourselves wrong. What is more, we can use Alexander's discovery as a guide to progress along the way.

Notes

1. In *Notes of Instruction* in *The Alexander Technique - the essential writings of F M Alexander* selected by Ed Maisel.

2. Please refer to pg 172, *Escape from the Monkey Hatch* by Don Weed, where we find: "If you stop the wrong thing from happening, the right thing happens by itself," and also: "...I found something said to me by Margaret Goldie to be of some interest. She said that F.M. used to say, "You don't have to "do" anything. All you have to do is stop the wrong thing from taking place and the thing you want to happen will take place because you are perfectly made.""

3. See 2 above.

4. Taken from notes of Don Weed teaching in the UK.

5. pg 78, *Constructive Conscious Control of the Individual.*

6. pg 36, *The Use of the Self.*

7. pg 265, *If you want to be rich and happy, don't go to school.*

8. *Psycho-cybernetics* by Maxwell Maltz

9. *The Artist's Way* by Julia Cameron

10. According to Marjory Barlow (Aphorisms, published in "Direction", vol. 2,6 / Memorial Lecture 1995, published in "Alexander Journal" no. 15.

Navigating Reefs and Rocks

"They prevent the ideals in which they say they believe from materializing by the principles on which they work."

F M Alexander

The first three principles in conjunction with Alexander's discovery provide us with a foundation for bringing about ongoing and lasting improvements in our general standard of performance. They can help us get better at whatever it is we do. The next three principles relate to major pitfalls in learning the work. In this section, I will tell you about pot-holes in the road. I need to do this because what almost all students without exception do, when presented with the wherewithal to move forward, is to sabotage their progress. Instead of cultivating the discipline necessary to work to these basic principles in the daily round of their lives, the overwhelming majority of students now place obstacles in their way. They do this by employing principles guaranteed to impede progress, principles that will almost certainly run their ship aground. You may not, but these chapters are here to let you know of the mistakes others have made, so that you can avoid them, so that you can successfully navigate the major reefs and rocks on this voyage.

Four

From One Extreme to Another

mistaking effects for causes

"'Don't do this, but this,' says the teacher, dealing with effects. In other words, it is assumed that the defective action on the part of the pupil can be put right by 'doing something else.'"
- F M Alexander[1]

"It is owing to this habit of rushing from one extreme to another, to this tendency, that is, to take the narrow and treacherous side-tracks instead of the great, broad midway path, that our plan of civilization has proved a comparative failure."

F M Alexander [2]

In 1996, my son, Leif, was born. In the weeks and months that followed his early operation, I ran through my mind all the things I could remember of my own early years, of the things I had liked and had not. (So many years had by then passed, I have no idea how reliable my memories were, but certain memories were recurring.) And, as if often the case with parents nowadays, it was things I remembered happening to me that I didn't like which surfaced first.

In the beginning, I thought I remembered being left alone to scream myself to sleep, of crying out as loud as I could and no one coming. Next, I thought I remembered my Dad not being there, of wanting to see him and being unable.

In all likelihood, events like these probably happened, even if I had later invented the memories and accompanying feelings rather than actually having them. I now know my Dad was working seven days a week, having used all his holiday leave to be present at my birth on account of my being extremely over-due; and common wisdom in the sixties was that babies should be left to sleep alone, irrespective of their screams and tears.

Like many new parents, my instinctive reaction to these 'memories' was to seek to ensure Leif had the opposite experience from me. I would make sure he was never left alone to scream himself to sleep, and that I would spend as much time as possible with him in his early years.

In other new parents, I have seen a similar phenomenon. For example, I have known several parents who have looked back and remembered what they considered to be too much discipline, too many rules, which they have equated with their own difficulties in expressing themselves. As a consequence, they have given their own children free rein to do pretty much anything they please.

In Leif's case, at the age of five, he is extremely reluctant to go to sleep on his own, just as a young mother I know is now having to exert more force than I thought she possessed to impose rules on a once rule-less boy.

I have no desire to argue for the rights or wrongs of the different approaches to bringing up children outlined here; I wish only to comment on thinking involved in the *switch*. I call it, following F M Alexander, going from one extreme to another; in the ITM, we refer to the principle involved in this transaction as, 'the opposite of a fault is the same fault.'

The enemy of my enemy is not neccessarily my friend.

As it happens, F M Alexander was highly interested in the education of of children. We know that he even set up his own school so that children could be taught according to his principles. (Sadly, the school he set up in England had to close on account of the Second World War.)

It occurs to me that if people of my generation, born in the sixties, think they were subjected to too much discipline, it is hard to conceive the extent to which Victorian children were coerced and controlled. From what I have read, the experience is beyond our imaginings. It is documented that the parents of poorer children would often keep them out of school, fearful of the extreme physical punishments meted out. In private schools, if the account of Winston Churchill is to be believed, the situation was little different.

By the 1920's, in Britain and in America, a new movement in

children's education was beginning to emerge: namely, Free Expression, or the Free School approach. One of Alexander's American students, the philosopher and educationalist, John Dewey, was at the forefront of it. In Free Schools (according to F M), children were freed from outside interference or restraint. They were given materials and encouraged to express themselves without guidance or precept. To my initial surprise, Alexander was opposed. However, a closer reading of the objections he voices in *Man's Supreme Inheritance* enabled me to comprehend his reasoning.

According to F M, the proponents of free expression had simply gone from one wrong idea to its opposite. Believing that A was bad, they concluded that *not A* had to be good. F M thought differently. For him, if A is bad, then we must seek to eliminate the cause of A, or the conditions that enable it to flourish. In the educational context, if excessive discipline and rigid instruction were associated with people being unable to express themselves, the solution was not to abandon rules or instruction, but rather to seek out and eradicate the actual cause.

F M believed that the problem was caused neither by instruction nor by discipline; the problem was that children had not been taught or supported in the art of expressing themselves. To do this, F M believed that both rules and instruction were important; he also believed, just as my Dad did, in encouraging children to think for themselves.

> *"From one extreme [the advocates of free expression] have flown to the other, and so have missed the way of the great middle course which is wide enough to accommodate all shades of opinion."*
>
> *F M Alexander*[3]

The thinking involved in going from one extreme to another crops up just about everywhere. We see it in people's attempts to improve their health, their love-life, their jobs, their children. We see it in so much of the research published in newspapers and magazines. Almost everyone goes for the effect, the symptom. Almost no one will root out the cause and go to work there.

As F M Alexander wrote: "In every sphere of life we have for years given 'effects' the significance of 'causes' and have

"Give a child poise and the reasoned control of his physical being, and you fit him for any and every mode of life." - F M Alexander

made worthy attempts to put matter right on this unsound basis."[4]

Should any of my readers doubt this, let me list some of the many examples I have come across, and tell me if you don't recognize the thinking in yourself.

How many of us, when we come down with a cold, take drugs that we know only suppress symptoms, yet persuade ourselves we are effecting a cure?

Likewise, how many of us, when we are in pain, look for anything that will make the pain disappear, rather than investigate the actual cause? As a consequence, if our doctor prescribes a pain-killer, and the pain goes away, we convince ourselves we have (at least temporarily) been cured.

How many people do you know who, after a failed relationship, choose a partner who seems to be (on the surface) the complete opposite of the last?

How many parents do you know who, when the carrots they offer their children don't work, do an immediate u-turn and offer them sticks?

If you follow politics, you will surely recognize that, after every lost election, there is almost always a loud voice from within the ranks of the losing party advocating an exact reversal of policy on key election issues. For example, at the last General Election in Britain, the Conservative Party supposedly lost the votes of young people because of its intolerance towards illegal drugs. Within weeks of defeat, a number of leading voices on the far right of the party were advocating legalizing all drugs.

Likewise, every time the English football team loses an international, there are commentators who immediately advocate the team do exactly the opposite of whatever they did last time. If the team tried to pass the ball, next time they should kick the ball forward into space. If x played, next time they should use y; if y played, next time they should use x. In each case, the strategy advocated may or may not help, but the point is the failure to seek out the cause and address it. What we all-too-often see is an instinctive knee-jerk reaction that results in lurching from one extreme to the next.

Seemingly every time I read the newspaper there is evidence that this or that food or lifestyle choice causes this or that health problem. In each and every case, the only evidence cited consists in researchers identifying associations. For example, we are told that people who live in the South of England live longer than those living in the North, with the result that we are advised, if we live in the North, to up sticks and head South. In much the same way, we are given endless injunctions about what we should and should not eat, according to what researchers have succeeded in associating with ill-health, with the result that the advice we are given changes year by year.

Similarly, it is precisely this failure of reasoning that has led many young people to reject reasoning as a principle for improvement, on account of their having made an association between people's attempts at employing reasoning in the past with our current problems in the world. A great many people of my generation have looked around them and thought: "All these scientific and technological advances, and what good has it done?" They have seen environmental devastation, nuclear bombs and biological weapons, let alone millions upon millions of children still going needlessly hungry. As a consequence, they have thought: "So much reason and reasoning, and what good has it done?"

But to think in this way is indeed to mistake an association for a cause; to subsequently reject reasoning out of hand is to be guilty of, as we say, "throwing the baby out with the bath-water." For isn't it just as likely that our present difficulties are the result of our collective failure to bring the use of reason into how we use ourselves and our dealings with others? Is it not just as likely that our present difficulties have arisen because we have spent all our energy endeavouring to figure out how to make things work outside of us, and so little in how we use ourselves?

*

The thinking involved in going from one extreme to another is always associated with mistaking effects for causes. It involves attending to symptoms only, of not bothering to root out the actual cause. We could describe this habit of thought as a failure of reasoning, that is, a failure to think things through in relation to cause and effect. In the specific context of F M's disovery, it leads us to try to do the opposite of what we perceive to be wrong, rather than going to work as a first step to stop. So that, if we notice that we are pulling our head back and down, it leads us to push our head forward and up. Regrettably, however, this will not help us, for the opposite of a fault is still a fault.

One of my favourite images to remind myself of this principle is trying to fill the bath without a plug to stop the water draining away. But, instead of getting something to stop the plug-hole, I see myself turning on the taps full-blast, then getting more and more water from jugs and kettles, but to my dismay all my water keeps draining away. In this imaginary scenario, I act as if the the problem is not enough water, when in fact the problem is no plug to stop it draining away. In class, I see the same thing happen frequently: students often act as if the problem is their bodies, when the real power lies in their ideas.

Go back to first principles. Remember: the opposite of a fault is still a fault.

"If only I could my head-neck relationship sorted out," they say, twisting and turning their heads. "Go back to first principles," I say. "Remember: the opposite of a fault is still a fault."

In class, it is comparatively easy for me to demonstrate the principle of, 'from one extreme to the other,' and I am called upon to do so fairly often.

First, I ask my students to watch me. Then I raise my shoulders a few inches and keep them raised. I walk around the room and ask my students if they can imagine someone making the movement behaviour I am making practically all the time. They usually nod in agreement.

Then I ask my students if they can imagine somebody else

telling the character I am playing that he looks wrong, that he should try to lower his shoulders a few inches to look right. They nod their assent. (It is usually the case that many of them will have been given similar advice themselves, especially if, as children, they liked to slump in chairs.) Next, I pull my shoulders down. That is, rather than relax the muscles that are keeping them raised, I use another set of muscles to overpower the movement I am already making. In this way, I get my shoulders back down to where they originally were. To some observers, it looks as if I have succeeded in eradicating the original fault. I have got my shoulders back to where most the students think they ought to be. Except, I am now completely rigid across my chest. I am pulling my shoulders up and pulling them down. If I keep going long enough, I start to ache. Then I stop both movements simultaneously. To my students, although my shoulders do not go significantly up or down, I suddenly appear easy again across my chest. I breathe a sigh of relief and so do they.[5]

The first strategy I employ in this demonstration, when I pull my shoulders down, deals only with an effect. The second strategy, when I stop making the original movement, engages the cause. The first strategy highlights the principle of, "from one extreme to another." The original movement is still there; the cause has not been addressed.

In class, when I help students to work on their chosen activities, we regularly see this principle at work. Many students, after only a few lessons, reach the conclusion that it is a mistake to interfere with the relationship between head and body as they go into activity. The strategy they most often adopt is to keep their head firmly in place.

Unfortunately, by using this strategy, they have done nothing to address the cause or causes that give rise to movement behaviours they perceive a need to prevent. At no point have they considered the thinking that generates their unwanted movement behaviour. In practice, the (unreasoning) strategy they adopt usually makes matter worse, for they keep their heads in place by increasing rather than decreasing the amount of interference they create.

In this connection, one of students, Barry, is learning to play golf. To speed him along his way, he is taking lessons from a professional. Initially, Barry reported that he was making good progress. This last week, however, he came to see me complaining his game had suddenly got worse.

I asked him to show me his swing. I was immediately struck by an undue rigidity in his hips and knees. In my view, this was a recent addition, as I had not seen this excessive muscular activity when he showed me his swing some weeks before.

"What are you trying to do?" I asked.

"My teacher told me I was moving my left leg too much, so now I am trying to keep it still."

"Well done," I said. "If that's your goal, you are doing really well."

Unfortunately, the method Barry had adopted for keeping the leg in place involved the creation of so much muscular tension he could barely move his leg at all. Instead of ceasing to make what the professional judged to be an excessive movement, my student was keeping his leg fixed firmly in place. In so doing, he was ruining his swing, as he had radically curtailed his freedom to move.

"When you are asked not to do something, instead of making the decision not to do it, you try to prevent yourself from doing it. But this only means you decide to do it, and then use muscle tension to prevent yourself from doing it."

F M Alexander[6]

In the event, the left leg moving too much proved to be a symptom of a more general problem. For when I worked with Barry to stop overly tightening the muscles of his neck and back, the problem of the wayward left leg largely disappeared. Significantly, to get my student to stop tightening his muscles needlessly, I went to work on his ideas. Afterwards, he went to work with a new set of rules. From there on, in my view - and also that of the other students in the group - his swing got significantly better.

In this instance, my student has sought to eradicate the perceived fault by doing its opposite. He had done nothing to address the cause. He had indeed flown from one extreme to the other. In this, he was not exceptional. It is something just about all of us have done and continue to do. However, it is something we need to stop if we would raise our standard of performance in everything we do.

Likewise, a great many students experience a feeling they describe as lightness, or relaxation, during lessons. When feeling this way, they notice they are moving better, in the sense of performing at a higher standard with improved co-ordination. As a consequence, whenever they think they are performing poorly, many students will seek to create a feeling of relaxation in themselves. Unfortunately, what they have failed to recognize is that the feeling of relaxation in lessons comes about as an effect of their interfering less. It comes about as a result of a change in thinking. It is a merely a symptom and not the cause. So when students seek to solve their problem by "relaxing," what they invariably do is some other interference on top of the original one. They do things, as John Dewey said, "a different kind of badly."[7] When what they really need to do is to stop.

"Let us take for example the case of a man who habitually stiffens his neck in walking, sitting or other ordinary acts of life. [...] if he is told to relax those stiffened muscles of the neck and obeys the order, this mere act of relaxation deals only with an effect, and does not quicken his consciousness of the use of the right mechanism which he should use in place of those relaxed."

F M Alexander[8]

To attempt to bring about the desired improvement by addressing the effect only leaves the cause untouched. The original fault is still present, for, the opposite of a fault is indeed the same fault.

In Chapter 1, we concluded that we needed to go to work on the thinking that generates both what we do and how we do it. In other words, we would go to work on our ideas. In chapter 2, we identified a tool, a wonderful tool, for getting better: namely, the just use of conscious reason. And by that we meant, at least in part, thinking things through with an open mind. We meant engaging the conscious mind without imposing restrictions on the free play of the imagination. We meant, to use Alexander's words, "quickening the conscious mind."[9] In Chapter 3, we identified a supreme strategy for going to work: namely, the principle of prevention. We decided to go to work as if we were well-made.

But we cannot possibly succeed in working to these principles by doing the opposite of what we perceive to be wrong. On the contrary, we must stick with the thinking that generate our response. We must abandon all knee-jerk reactions. We must go to work on the cause.

If we are to build on our foundation, we must fully recognize the folly of going from one extreme to another; we must root out and go to work on the cause. To that end, we will go to work as if we are well-made by changing our thinking. We will abandon looking for something *to do* to stop.

Notes

1. pg 128, *Man's Supreme Inheritance.*
2. pg 64, *Constructive Conscious Control of the Individual.*
3. pg 84, *Man's Supreme Inheritance.*
4. pg 94, *Man's Supreme Inheritance.*
5. When muscles fire, they get shorter. For that reason, if a muscle is attached to two different bones that cross a joint, when the muscle fires, there will be movement at the joint. However, if the person simultaneously contracts an opposing set of muscles to counter the original movement, there will of course be no movment at the joint. In this way, we can either lock a joint by turning on opposing sets of muscles, or we can leave the joint alone by not switching on muscles. In both scenarios, there will be no movement at the joint.

To that end, in the absence of injury of disease, we recognise that stiffness at joints is caused by the overaction of muscles, whereas increased flexibility is evidence of a reduction in unnecessary muscular activity. In teaching Alexander's work, increased flexibility is evidence of improvement, as unintentional stiffness is symptomatic of interference in the right working of the mechanism.

6. *Notes of Instruction* in *The Alexander Technique - the essential writings of F M Alexander* edited by Ed Maisel.
7. Refer to *The Use of the Self.*
8. pg. 59, *Man's Supreme Inheritance.*
9. pg 33, *Man's Supreme Inheritance.*

Five

Feelings are Unreliable

on not using feelings as a guide

"Imagine yourself siting in a train at a railway station. It has been a long journey. You are hungry and thirsty. You are waiting for the buffet-car to open. You ask the guard, "When will the buffet open?" The guard assures you that the buffet car will open just as soon as the train leaves the station. The train doesn't move. Then, after what seems like an age, the train starts moving and you jump up. But, as you begin to run down the aisle, you realise that the train is in fact still stationary. It was a different train moving in the station that gave rise to the impression that your train was moving too."

"The belief is very generally held that if only we are told what to do in order to correct a wrong way of doing something, we can do it, and that if we feel we are doing it, all is well. All my experience, however, goes to show that this belief is a delusion."

F M Alexander[1]

This chapter is all about feelings. It addresses and rejects the idea of using feelings as a guide. In this chapter, I put forward the view that feelings are unreliable. My stance is unequivocal: feelings are unreliable. That's right: your feelings are unreliable. If you want to build on the foundations you have laid, you must abandon relying on your feelings as a guide.

Telling people their feelings are unreliable is provocative. It almost always produces a reaction the first time I say it in a class. For that reason, it is important I explain as clearly as possible what I mean, that I don't give you a reason for abandoning this journey because you think I am saying something I am not.

First, let's take a look at the word, "feeling." In his truly wonderful book, *Four Days In Bristol — an Introduction to the Interactive*

Teaching Method, Don Weed makes the following joke: "I feel that what I feel about the things that I feel when I feel something gives me really outrageous feelings."[2]

In that mind-boggling sentence, there must be at least four clearly different meanings of the word *feeling*, ranging from belief to impression to sensation to emotion.

In class, we hear people use the word in all these different ways; however, in the context of work on a specific activity, the most common usage of the word is interpretation of sensory data. For example, students will say: 'It feels like I'm leaning backwards'; or, 'I can feel my arms getting longer'; or, 'I now feel free across my chest.' When these students describe what they feel, they are giving an interpretation derived from sensory data. So, when I make the claim: "feelings are unreliable," I am saying that our interpretation of what is happening to us according to the information we receive via our senses is sometimes misleading. If it feels that our head is tipping forward, it does not mean that our head is tipping forward. If I feel my bum is sticking out, I may be wrong. If we feel we have stopped tightening the muscles in our necks, we may not have. As Alexander is reported to have said: "If your neck feels stiff, that is not to say your neck 'is' stiff."[3]

"I feel that what I feel about the things that I feel when I feel something gives me really outrageous feelings."

Don Weed

But why should our feelings mislead us? And, more to the point, in the context of improving the way we direct ourselves in activity, why does it matter?

The fact that feelings are unreliable matters because so many of us want to build on our foundation on the basis of our feelings. We want to judge relative success or failure in continuing this journey according to what and how we feel. However, what we feel is often a poor measure of what is actually happening, for the simple reason that our feelings are an unreliable guide.

Feelings are unreliable for two important reasons:

i) feelings are relative; and

ii) feelings are fashioned by ideas.

First, what does it mean to say that feelings are relative?

Well, at the beginning of this chapter, I asked you to imagine yourself in a stationary train at a railway station. In this scenario, you acquire the impression your train has started to move, only to discover that it was another train moving. In actuality, your train was stationary all along. I have yet to meet a student who has not been able to identify with this experience. People tell me they have this experience of moving when stationary all the time. They have it on buses, trains, boats, planes. Why? Because they were moving. Only not with respect to the road, the track, the water or the run-way, but with respect to something else that moved. That is how our feelings are. They are relative. They tell us about change from one state to another. They don't tell us about how things are in themselves; they inform us about relative change.

"If your neck feels stiff, that is not to say your neck is stiff."

F M Alexander

In class, the most common illustration of this principle occurs when students are working on activities that involve standing. If the student habitually leans backwards to stand, and I succeed in finding a way of getting them to stop, so that they look to me and the rest of the group to be more or less upright, the student will, in ninety-nine cases out of a hundred, tell me that they are now leaning forwards. For some, the experience is so dramatic, they are convinced they will fall flat on their faces unless I help them to stay up. For those watching, this presents an entertaining spectacle.

Why does this happen? Why do the students feel they are leaning forwards when in fact they are standing up straight? Because they are leaning forwards. Only with respect to how they were standing before and not with the ground. Feelings are relative.

They let us know that things are changing (or remaining the same); they do not tell us how things are in themselves.

If we are in a dark room and go into a even darker one, should we go back to the first room again, it suddenly appears to us light. If we have spent years locked up in a cell, then activities we previously took for granted, like walking down the street or sitting in the park, will often, upon our release, lead to an experience of freedom of staggering proportions. Similarly, if we have spent the last decade creating inordinate amounts of unnecessary muscular tension throughout our bodies, but so continuously that we are no longer able to feel it, then, when we stop, living can seem like heaven on earth. The sudden loss of tension can re-awaken a lust for life.

"Feelings are relative." It was the application of precisely this principle that led Einstein to develop relativity theory. And, as we all know, the idea of relativity is a dominant idea in the modern age. Some people, however, have taken the idea of relativity so far, they make the claim that there are no such things as facts. But that is not the idea I am presenting. On the contrary, my idea of relativity it simply that our interpretation of how things are changing (or have changed) will always depend on our initial point of view, that is, the place we started measuring from. When it comes to our feelings in the sense of our interpretation of sensory data, we measure from the place we habitually are.

Feelings are relative. They are not absolute. They do not tell us how things are in themselves. For that reason they are unreliable. They can and do mislead us. If we seek to use them as a guide to how we are performing, we run the risk of making errors, particularly when it comes to acts we perform day in and day out. But feelings are unreliable not only because they are relative; feelings are unreliable because they are fashioned by our ideas. And, as I will soon argue, our fashioning ideas are frequently misleading.

But first, let's examine the notion that feelings are fashioned by ideas. To do this, we will take a brief look at the neuro-physiology of sensory impressions.

In chapter one, we made the claim that it is all but universally agreed that human movements are caused by the sending of messages from the motor cortex along nerves to the muscular mechanism. As it happens, there is just about the same level of agreement that our sensory experience of the world comes about as a result of processing information received by the brain from the senses. Basically, messages from receptors pass along nerves to the sensory cortex, where they are somehow transformed into the sensory experience we have of our world.

My claim is that, just as the sending of motor messages is directed by thinking, so to is the processing of sensory data. The interpretation we make of the information we receive from our senses is governed by our ideas. My claim is that we filter and make sense of the sensory information we receive in a manner both governed by and directed by our ideas.*

"Feelings are fashioned by ideas."

Here's an example:

I live within 200 yards - that's 180m to my European friends - of Bristol University's Will's Memorial Building, a huge, gothic tower built on the top of a hill. From the hours of seven in the morning till 9 o'clock at night, a loud, booming bell situated in the top of the tower chimes out the time every hour on the hour: one chime for each hour of the day.

When I first moved to my current home, this bell would wake me in the mornings, and I would frequently hear the bells throughout the day. These days, however, I almost never hear

*   Consequently, when we make the claim that feelings are unreliable, we are not claiming that our sensory mechanism is somehow at fault; only that the interpretation we make of our sensory data is fashioned by potentially misleading ideas.

them. I am not woken by the chimes, nor does the clanging punctuate the hours of my day, as it did when I first moved to Bristol. I only ever seem to hear the chimes now when I'm hungry, when a single, solitary clang lets me know it is time to stop writing and to eat.

What has changed? Certainly not the bells. Every newcomer claims to hear them. No, something in me has changed. And if you ask what in me, then I will tell you it is my thinking, my ideas.

These days, it is as if I can no longer bother to either make sense of or even record the noise. Unless, there's something in it for me. Unless I want to eat, or, as happened recently, I've forgotten to set my alarm-clock and I need to wake up. Then, I hear them loud and clear. Make no mistake. (Coincidentally, it's just started chiming now.) The only thing that has changed here is me. Not the bells; not my auditory mechanism. I make a different interpretation of the sound impressions I receive simply because my ideas about their significance have changed. When I first got here, I paid serious attention. Now, most of the time, I hear no clanging at all. Except, when I change my mind, when I change my ideas about their relative importance. Then, and only then, do I find myself hearing the bells.

"Okay, so maybe our interpretation of sensory data is in fact fashioned by our ideas. But that doesn't make our feelings unreliable. It just means we are selective about what we feel. Right?"

Unfortunately, no. Our feelings are fashioned by our ideas, and these ideas are frequently misleading. Here's another example.

Many years ago, before I had set up Gil, I had a job as a trainer for the youth service, and I specialized in drugs and sex education. One day, I was in the office planning a course with my boss, when a guard from the local prison walked in. I forget his name, so let me call him Alf.

It turned out Alf was a worried man. A very worried man. A few days ago, Alf had been involved in a fracas with a prisoner, during which, so Alf believed, he might have been bitten. Nothing so unusual about that, you might think. Except, as Alf went on to say, shortly after the struggle, this particular prisoner, a known intravenous drug user, claimed he had AIDS.

Back then, in the late eighties, there was enormous prejudice and confusion concerning HIV and AIDS. Many people believed it was possible to contract HIV from casual contact, let alone biting, and Alf was one of these people. He wanted to know everything we knew, and what he could do to save his life, and the lives of the people around him.

My boss set about reassuring Alf. Even if the prisoner was HIV+, even if Alf had in fact been bitten, the chances he had contracted the virus were very slim. And even if by some remarkable sequence of events he had in fact contracted the virus, he could not pass it onto his family by touching them, or by sharing the same knives and forks, or even by kissing. Alf went away, armed with leaflets and books, seemingly reassured. However, he would take a blood test just to be sure.

"It doesn't alter a fact because you can't feel it."

F M Alexander

The next time we met Alf, he told us a remarkable story. Although Alf had come to the conclusion that he almost certainly had not contracted the virus, within a few days of our meeting, he began to develop a number of distressing symptoms. Each time he read about a possible symptom marking the onset of AIDS, he subsequently acquired the symptom himself. He would wake up in a cold sweat; or he would get stomach cramps; or he would experience pains in his neck or under his arms, which he was sure meant his lymph glands had become swollen, and that his immune system was about to fail. In the event, it was not until Alf had taken a blood test which proved negative that all his symptoms disappeared. It was only then that he slept comfortably again.[4]

I tell Alf's story to illustrate the fact that we are able to distort, diminish, amplify or even fabricate feelings in ourselves.

In this connection, my son, Leif, will often not feel any pain after a fall until he sees blood. And from that moment on, the pain can seem more than he can bear.

Everyone has heard of the placebo effect. We know that a doctor can give a depressed patient a sugar pill telling him it is Prozac, and the patient will frequently report an improvement in his condition. The patient is not lying. He or she really does feel better. Likewise, how often do we feel better when we do something which we believe is good for us, even if it is later proven that the activity has no beneficial effect? In my experience, a great deal of the time.

In class, we see this phenomenon repeatedly. For example, if a musician is asked to stop doing something they believe they need to do to play well, and they succeed in stopping, they will often report that they are now playing worse, even if the rest of the group and the teacher observe a significant improvement. To the student, the music really does sound worse. According to the intensity of their conviction, they will decide that everyone else is right or wrong, and keep or change their point of view.

As a consequence of these experiences, I tell my students, just because you feel something, it doesn't mean it is true. As David Burns writes: "feelings are not facts."[5] If we feel we are moving better, it doesn't mean we are. If we feel we are moving worse, it doesn't mean we are. In many cases, we have reasons for feeling what we feel, and these reasons have little to with how things actually are, but everything to do with what we believe. Our interpretation of our sensory impressions is governed by our thoughts and our convictions. Our feelings are indeed fashioned by our ideas. And many of our ideas are false.

"Okay, so maybe our feelings are unreliable. But what has that to do with me?"

If you want to improve: lots.

In the course of my work as a teacher of Alexander's technique, I have discovered that the tendency to decide whether or not we are making progress according to how we feel is practically universal. In the early days of lessons, the temptation to decide whether or not we have succeeded in stopping according to what we feel is all but irresistible. If the student feels better, the student convinces herself she is better; if a student feels worse, the student convinces himself he is worse. But, because I know that feelings are unreliable, it is my responsibility as the teacher to get some independent proof before reaching a conclusion. In all cases, what the student reports they feel will only every be suggestive of what is happening. I will always look to see how the student performs as well. I will always seek objective evidence. And I will ask my students to do the same. I will ask them to re-consider the value of changing what they are doing according to what and how they feel.

"Feelings are not facts."

David Burns

One of my students – I'll call him Sid – always seems to get a dull, aching pain in his shoulder every time he makes what I, and the rest of the class, think of as an improvement. As soon as Sid stops tying himself up in particular way, he moves a whole lot better. But Sid always gets this ache as well. Relying on his feelings, Sid is tempted to go back to the earlier, ache-free condition. Relying on the feedback of the group, Sid is minded to accept the feeling and not act on it.* In this way, Sid is able to make progress. He does not seek to rely on his feelings. He looks outside himself for evidence of progress.

*   It seems likely that Sid ties himself up to get rid of the ache, which has some other, as yet unknown, cause.

In this connection, you may remember that Alexander decided to make use of a mirror to see what he did in reciting. He did not feel himself to be pulling his head back and down, but he was. His feelings were unreliable. I make a point of telling all my students this story. Yet a great many of them will - just as Alexander confesses he did, and as I did myself - assume they have stopped making a movement behaviour they wish to prevent because they cannot feel it. This, despite the fact that previous lessons have demonstrated that their interpretation of sensory data is misleading.

Many students believe that they have stopped pulling their heads backwards as they go into activity because they no longer feel it. However, they are making this judgment using a mechanism which has proved itself defective in the past. They never felt themselves to be doing so before, so why should they trust their sense of feeling now?[6]

In view of this everyday teaching experience, Alexander writes:

"The belief is very generally held that if only we are told what to do in order to correct a wrong way of doing something, we can do it, and that if we feel we are doing it, all is well. All my experience, however, goes to show that this belief is a delusion."[7]

A great many students want to build on their foundation according to their feelings. However, our feelings are an untrustworthy guide. Therefore, we must instead look for objective evidence of improvement. In practice, this means we will have to assess how the student in question performs. Following Alexander, we can view improvements in the dynamic relationship of head to body in movement as indicative of improvements in our general standard of co-ordination; we can use the student's general standard of performance as a more effective and reliable guide.

*

We will build on our foundation not by seeking to do the opposite of what we perceive to be wrong; nor will we judge our relative success according to how or what we feel. No, we will instead engage our minds with the task of changing our thinking to stop sending ourselves wrong. In doing this, we will look for objective evidence of success or failure. We will give up seeking to use feelings as a guide.

Notes

1. pg 33, *The Use of Self*.
2. pg 17, *Four Days in Bristol* by Don Weed
3. In *Notes of Instruction* in *The Alexander Technique - the essential writings of F M Alexander* edited by Ed Maisel.
4. Alf told us that the whole experience had forced upon him the realisation that he and the other prison officers were woefully ignorant about HIV. After reading the books and other information we had given him, he quickly realised that there was no need to segregate prisoners suspected of having the disease. They could be returned to the main prison population without significant risk. However, this would require education all the officers and inmates, a task which he willingly undertook to do himself, and with which, I am happy to say, we were able to assist him. Incidentally, some time later the prison was praised as model for good practice in HIV and AIDS education.
5. Please refer to *Feeling Good* by David Burns, MD.
6. The person who thinks in this way is just like the person who returns to buy a second copy of a newspaper to check for a misprint in the first. (This metaphor comes from Wittgenstein's *Philosophical Investigations*.)
7. pg 33, *The Use of the Self*.

Six
Fixed, Preconceived Ideas
paradigms, preconceptions and prejudice

"She was never one to let facts get in the way of her reality."

A woman returns to her optician. She takes off the spectacles she is wearing and throws them onto the counter. "These glasses are useless," she says. "They haven't improved my sight at all. I see worse with them than without. I want my money back."

"I'm very sorry, Madame," says the optician. "Let me test them."

The optician picks up the spectacles and examines them carefully. Then he puts them on and stares at the woman. "I'm sorry, but Madame is mistaken," he says. "They seem perfectly fine to me."

*

We all see the world differently. We all have our own unique set of beliefs. Some ideas are shared by our friends and colleagues; others serve to differentiate us. Similarly, we all move differently: no two walks are exactly alike, just as everyone's hand-writing and speech-patterns are different. In certain respects, we are more like some than others; in others, we are more different. We all have, according to F M Alexander, a unique psycho-physical make-up.

These days, the word most often used to describe beliefs

associated with different ways of seeing the world is *paradigm*. According to Stephen Covey:

"The word *paradigm* comes from the Greek. It was originally a scientific term, and is more commonly used today to mean a model, theory, perception, assumption, or frame of reference. In the more general sense, it's the way we "see" the world – not in terms of our visual sense of sight, but in terms of perceiving, understanding, interpreting."[1]

In this sense, paradigms relate to models or maps.

In fiction, we are talking about the same thing when we say that each character has a particular *point of view*. In practice, the narrative voice is almost always sustained by a single point of view, that is, a particular take on the world. For the reader, the point of view defines the character. As the story develops, we get to "see" the world through his or her eyes.

"A changed point of view is the royal road to reformation."

F M Alexander

In the ITM, we make the claim that there is a relationship between thinking and movement in which thinking is causal. We also claim that we act in accordance with our paradigms, so that, the way a person behaves tells us about how they *see* the world. To that extent, if a person wants to improve their general standard of performance, then their *take* on things will have to change. They will need to embrace new paradigms. They will need to adopt a changed point of view. As F M Alexander wrote in *Man's Supreme Inheritance*: "a changed point of view is the royal road to reformation."[2]

In practice, we find that students come to Alexander's work with a variety of more or less fixed points of view, and to that extent they attempt to continue the journey according to their fixed ideas. They may well grasp the idea that they must work to change their thinking to stop sending themselves wrong in the performance of each and every task; however, their efforts to do this are hampered by their attachment to paradigms that are fixed. They want to employ Alexander's technique according to their current point of view, and thus miss the obvious next step forward.

In teaching my improvement class, I have consistently found that certain paradigms are associated with freedom and flexibility, while others occasion restriction and stiffness. For example, people who believe that stooping is caused by not tightening the muscles of the back sufficiently, are invariably stiffer than people who believe stooping is caused by too much tightening of the muscles on the front.

There are many, many fixing paradigms, that is, beliefs that diminish our freedom to move. However, in this chapter, I am less concerned with paradigms that are fixing than I am with paradigms that are fixed. Let me explain.

The student who has wrong ideas that he is little attached to is in practice much easier to teach than the student who has better ideas that are fixed. For the student with fixed ideas, that is, ideas that are not open to question, ideas that the student clings to with a mindless zeal, cannot possibly improve. To get better, the student must be willing to change. And that means they must be prepared to give up their pre-existing ideas. They must be willing to change their preconceptions, to relinquish their cherished beliefs. As F M Alexander wrote in his second book:

"If people go on believing that they 'know', it is important to eradicate anything: it makes it impossible to teach them."

F M Alexander

"A teaching experience of over twenty-five years in a psycho-physical sphere has given my a very real knowledge of the psycho-physical difficulties which stand in the way of many adults who need re-education and co-ordination, and, as a result of this experience, I have no hesitation in stating that the pupil's fixed ideas and conceptions are the major cause of his difficulties."[3]

In teaching, I have found – just as Alexander predicted - that students construe lessons according to their peculiar psycho-physical make-up. They reach conclusions about what it is they are being taught according to their pre-existing beliefs. And in order to have any chance of success, I must find a way of tempting them to look at things differently; I must help them make what Stephen Covey (following Thomas Kuhn) calls a paradigm shift.[4]

Here's an example.

Some months ago, a new student returned one week after her first lesson furious with me.

"You told me to put my head here," she said. "I've been doing that all week and now I'm worse than I was before. I've got pain in my neck as well as my back."*

I tried to explain that I had said no such thing. To no avail.

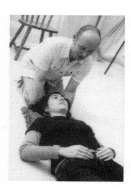

In the event, it wasn't until I was able to show her, using my hands, the difference between *relationship* and *position* with regard to her head and neck, with the result that the new pain disappeared, that she believed me. Despite my having repeated many times in her first lesson that I was not talking about the position of her head, she convinced herself that I had to be. As far as heads were concerned, in her world, position was everything: *position* was king.

In all likelihood, she had never before considered the idea of the relationship of her head to her body, and as a consequence had glossed over my remarks as being irrelevant insofar as her problems were concerned. Unfortunately, by so doing, she had succeeded in making her problems worse.

This student - like so many of us – had come to her first lesson with a preconceived idea about the importance of position with regard to her pain. She seemed never to have considered the idea of relationship, yet she had, in this extremely important matter of position versus relationship, arrived at a fixed idea. The way I saw it, it was my job as her teacher to give her reasons for loosening her attachment to her preconception. It was my job to help her to make a paradigm shift. In her case, the sudden absence of pain persuaded her to re-consider her prejudice,

* Just by looking at her, I could see she was holding her head rigidly fixed in one particular place.

with the result that she softened her attachment to the idea of position, and began to consider relationship instead.

In telling this anecdote, I am reminded of my own early difficulties in learning the technique. Back in 1995, when I first started having private lessons with John Gil, on those weeks when I thought about what he was saying, I got worse. That's right, on those occasions when, as far as I was concerned, I was in fact "studying the relationship between thinking and movement," when I did what I labeled "studying", I got worse. There were no two ways about it. Not only did I feel worse, but I was worse. I moved less well; my general standard of performance went down. I've seen the same thing happen to many beginning students. When they don't "think" about the work, they get better; when they do, they get worse.

Trust me, this can be a really awful place to be in. You want to understand, you want to learn, you long to improve, but all your attempts at engaging with the ideas send you backwards. I was experiencing what Robert Kiyosaki calls the "frustration" of learning.[5]

My big breakthrough came when I was able to link up something that I had read in Frank Pierce Jones' book, *Freedom to Change*, with an experience I had when having a lesson with John. The passage in question was: "My big stumbling block lay in my concept of thinking. Thinking meant narrowing the attention on a small point and keeping it there."[6]

The experience I had was in trying to answer a question I was being asked by John.

On this particular occasion, I found myself unable to do the thinking I believed I needed to do while John had his hands on my neck. In order to do what I labeled "thinking," it was as if I had to tighten the muscles in the back of my neck. My problem was that John had his hands on me in such a way that I couldn't easily tighten them. I experienced it as John not allowing me to think. I wanted to get rid of his hands so that I could do what

"My big stumbling block lay in my concept of thinking. Thinking meant narrowing the attention on a small point and keeping it there."

Frank Pierce Jones

I called "thinking" and answer the question.

And then it dawned on me: I was suffering from a delusion. Just like Frank Jones, I had a preconceived idea about what thinking was. So long as I held on to it, I was stopping myself from moving forward. I had to let go of my long-held belief.

Seemingly miraculously, I stopped doing something to think, and just *thought*. It didn't feel like thinking as I had come to know it. I wasn't making it happen by some effort of will. I was just thinking. Differently. I found I could answer John's question without trouble. I had made my own paradigm shift.

I don't know for how many years I had laboured under the mistaken belief that thinking about something involved some kind of physical effort. What I do know is that I got myself into the habit of doing something to myself to think. I wouldn't have described it as narrowing my attention as Frank did; for me, it was more like shutting things out, as if by doing so I could create a quiet place in my mind to reflect. But the transaction was exactly the same. I was limiting my capacity for engaging my mind by doing what I labeled "engaging" it. The solution lay in letting go of my fixed, preconceived idea. And as I let go of it, there was an improvement in my general standard of performance. Without doubt, I immediately began to improve.

*

In teaching Alexander's work, we find that students will (unless forced to do otherwise) build on the foundation they have laid according to their fixed, preconceived ideas. Invariably, their first efforts at moving forward are hampered by their attachment to ideas they have barely (if ever) considered.

The number of fixed ideas we encounter in teaching is all but limitless. There are, however, a number of fixed ideas that recur with such regularity that it worth well spending time to consider them. As F M Alexander wrote:

Certain [...] fixed ideas are encountered in the case of

almost every pupil; fixed ideas, for example, as to what constitutes the right and what the wrong method of going to work as a pupil; fixed ideas in regard to the necessity for concentration, if success is to attend the efforts of pupil and teacher; also a fixed belief [...] that, if a pupil is corrected for a defect, he should be taught *to do something* in order to correct it, instead of being taught, as a first principle, *how to prevent (inhibition) the wrong thing from being done.*[7]

Just as Alexander predicted, I, too, have encountered certain recurring, fixed ideas in teaching his work. And just like Alexander, I would like to spend some time examining them.

First, let us take a look at the idea that if something is wrong, then the pupil should be taught something to do to correct it. This idea should be familiar. We talked about it in Chapter 3, when we decided we would go to work as if we were well-made. We decided we would work to the principle of prevention, that we would seek as a first step to stop.

For many students, the principle of prevention, along with Don Weed's associated idea of well-madeness, is attractive. It is an idea, as we say, whose "time has come." Unfortunately, what I have found in teaching this principle is that although a great many students accept it in theory, less are able to apply it in practice. Why? Because a great many of them stick with their preconceived idea, (regardless of their stated intention).

For example: let's suppose I say to a beginning student, "This time, I'd like to see what happens if you stop pulling your head back as you begin to recite." What I will often find is that the student will fix their head in place. Why? Because they are still convinced of the need to do something; because they stick with their preconceived idea.

If I explain to the student that there is a world of difference between stopping pulling the head back on the one hand, and keeping it rigidly in place on the other, many will, upon thinking the matter over, say, "Why yes, of course!"

"Shall we have another go?" I might suggest.

"Yes, but first, tell me what I can do to stop."

"I'm not sure I follow you."

"Well, I see that I shouldn't try to fix my head in place, so what should I do?"

"Nothing."

"Yes, but how? How does one *do* nothing?"

"You don't do anything. You give up. You stop."

At this point, the student may well look lost and forlorn. They are so dominated by their fixed idea, they are so convinced of the need to do something, that they can only imagine stopping as an activity in itself.

In the event, in the very first lesson, I almost always have to *show* the student what is involved in stopping by using my hands. I help them to stop by giving them reasons to change their thinking. I do this by engaging their ideas – and I appreciate this may seem paradoxical - with my hands. In this way, I help them to loosen their attachment to their preconception. You could say, I help them to take a step in the direction of open-mindedness.

*

Some people are convinced of the need to do something to stop; others – as I was - of the need to do something to think. In teaching, I found yet another, related idea.

In class, when I work with my hands, I will often ask students the question: "Same or different?" (Most students take this to be a question about their feelings.) In response, a small proportion will massively ratchet up the amount of unnecessary muscular tension in themselves. These students are convinced there is something to do to feel; and that if they *try harder* by switching more muscles on, they will be better able to answer my question. (I have found this conviction is often strongest in students who believe themselves to be physically insensitive.)

What these students almost always do is to render themselves incapable of sensing any changes in themselves, apart from the tension they have just created. For students such as these, I have found it better to ask the group: "Same or different?" And then wait for the student to notice changes in themselves.

A lesser version of this same idea is demonstrated when the student closes their eyes to answer the "same or different" question. They too betray a belief in the idea that there is something to do to feel. These same people will, as a consequence of their conviction, if they try to "get in touch with their feelings," increase the amount of distortion in themselves. They genuinely believe they can become more sensitive to their feelings if they do something to themselves. However, there is nothing to do to feel. In fact, all my experience goes to support the idea that we are better able to sense ourselves when we stop doings things to ourselves. It deepens my conviction in the idea that we are well-made.

As F M wrote, what most people refer to as concentration is nothing more than: "a harmful condition of the body sustained by repeated orders from the objective mind."

A related but far more prevalent prejudice is to be found in connection with a student's conviction in the value of (so-called) concentration. A great many students believe that success in any psycho-physical activity can only be brought about by the use of concentration. In order to sing better, to walk better, to juggle better, to listen better, then they must employ what they refer to as concentration.

However, if we try the experiment – as F M recommends[8] – of asking people to demonstrate what they mean by concentration, then what they invariably demonstrate is nothing more than a variety of physical (and hence, by inference, mental) distortions. We see furrowed brows, squinted eyes, lop-sided heads, fixed chests, clenched legs and stupefied stares. As F M wrote, what most people refer to as concentration is nothing more than: "a harmful condition of the body sustained by repeated orders from the objective mind."[9]

It has been my experience that of all the fixed ideas a teacher of Alexander's work must attack, this belief in the value of concentration is one of the most damaging. For it should be clear from the preceding chapters that how a student chooses to organize their thinking to perform tasks is paramount in terms of their eventual success or failure. And if a student continues to organize their thinking on the basis of a fixed, preconceived idea about the value of concentration (as they conceive it), then they ensure that they stick with their existing way of directing themselves in activity. They commit themselves to trying even harder in exactly the same old way.

In fact, so deep and widespread is the prejudice regarding the need for concentration, that almost everyone will, if asked to pay attention to someone or something, begin to make themselves stiff. I have noted that for many people the only evidence that will persuade them that a child is listening to them is visible stiffness. They look for the absence of movement in the expression on the child's face; they look to see the head fixed firmly in place. People who are committed to a belief in the value of concentration when listening to instructions invariably look to children for a frown. They struggle to comprehend how someone could be paying attention with a smile.

The sad fact is that advocates of concentration invariably adopt a manner of thinking that is associated with a diminishment in their general standard of performance - something I have often observed in academics and engineers. Like a great many people who do so-called *thinking* jobs, they have a tendency to attribute success in their chosen field to their powers of concentration. So convinced are they of this, that they cannot conceive of a more beneficial way of thinking. They have built up such a deep conviction about the right way to think, that the idea of thinking differently to get better results initially makes little appeal.

However, experience shows that even if someone can demonstrate success in attending to a single train of thought by employing a stiffening they refer to as concentration, they almost always run into immediate difficulty when asked to add in a second or a third train, let alone a fourth or a fifth. Yet these same people recognize perfectly well that success in life – whether in the home, the office, or even in love - requires an ability to attend to more than one thing at once. It has been my repeated experience that the use of so-called concentration makes this task ever more difficult. For this reason if no other, it is my job to help them to abandon this particular, preconceived idea.

*

The last set of fixed beliefs I wish to address are those we have about ourselves.

In this connection, it seems that the great majority of students I have worked with have a more or less fixed idea about themselves insofar as their abilities and potentialities are concerned. However, if they want to get better, if they want to improve, it stands to reason that their old ideas about themselves, about what is possible or within easy reach, will have to perish.

In practice, this is what lessons on specific activities do best – they serve to undermine the students' preconceptions about themselves. When we work on activities like walking, talking, dancing, singing, students are forced to deal with facts that do not conform to the preconceived idea they have of themselves.

Students will often start out telling me that they are poorly co-ordinated, that their memory is lousy, that they cannot balance on one leg, that they cannot think of more than one thing at the same time, that they have no original ideas. In class, I have the great privilege of getting to stand in the way of these preconceptions, and asking them to consider their beliefs afresh. I give them reasons for loosening their attachment to their fixed ideas about themselves. You could say, I work towards helping them to adopt a more flexible self-image.

In my experience, it begins early, this process of deciding what we can and cannot do well.

The other day, I happened to ask Leif how he was enjoying P.E. (physical education) at school. Not so much, it transpired, and he proceeded to tell me why. Apparently, his confidence had just been dented: P.E. was no longer something he did well. When I asked why, he told me that they had been practising jumping over a rope, and this was something he just couldn't do. As a consequence, he had come to think he was no good at P.E. anymore. I tried to offer some words of encouragement, but with little success.

A few days later, I inquired again. This time, his confidence was high: P.E. was something he could do well. I wondered had he managed to jump over the rope, but no, it turned out the teacher had decided to abandon rope-jumping as an activity, and had gone back to activities at which he believed himself to be one of the best.

Sadly, a great many of us – often as young as Leif - came to conclusions about our abilities on the basis of tiny amounts of evidence. Over time, we came to fix these beliefs about ourselves. Unlike Leif, however, we never had a compelling enough reason to revise our all-too-hasty estimation, and so we decided we knew where our limits were. Possibly someone told us we weren't that clever, and we believed them. Perhaps we asked someone to dance and they said no, and so we imagined we looked ugly. Maybe we never got to see anyone who looked like us reaching the top of our chosen field, and so we ruled out the possibility without further investigation. Whatever the reason, people do decide (often erroneously) what they can and cannot achieve. And all-too-quickly their prejudice becomes fixed, that is, they fix it for themselves.

It is as if the idea of delaying reaching a final judgement about ourselves and our abilities is too much for most of us to bear. We want to able to draw a line in the sand, to fix our peg in the ground, to say this is who and what we are. "I can do this, but I can't do that, and I'll never, ever be able to do that." For whatever reason, we want the boundaries of our abilities to remain fixed. However, in teaching Alexander's work we find a student's general standard of performance is far from fixed. In fact, once they have mastered the understanding and skills necessary to move forward, the most serious obstacle to further progress is almost always a fixed idea about what they can and cannot achieve. Many people don't mind getting a little better, so long as it's not too much. Why? Because then they'd have to change the fixed idea they have of themselves; an idea which, over time, has come to give them a sense of who they are. Abandoning it would be like taking a step into a strange and foreign land. However, a flexible self-image is vital if we want to get better. We must have flexibility in our paradigms if we are to improve.

We must have flexibility in our paradigms if we are to improve.

But let's go back to Leif for a moment; as it happens, he is convinced he can't ride his bicycle without stabilizers. To date, I have not yet succeeded in getting him even to try. Whenever I suggest he gives it a go, he tells me that stabilizers are necessary for boys his size. In view of this, you may be surprised to learn that when Leif goes to the Downs with his bicycle, he can ride happily in a straight line without the stabilizers touching the ground. However, so convinced is he that he needs stabilizers to cycle, I am reasonably confident that if I were to take them off, and he tried to ride without them, he'd fall off his bike immediately. He would run into the preconceived idea he has of himself. *Bang!*

In class, teachers of Alexander's work are always running up against preconceptions about what students can and cannot do. In this, students are like Leif with his stablilizers. Often, everyone else in the group sees a particular student perform at a higher standard without help; everyone else sees the potential for huge, independent improvement, but the student in question stubbornly persists with their false idea. "I know I did it then, but I can't do it again," they say; or, "I can only do it well when I am helped." They stubbornly cling to their fixed idea irrespective of what actually takes place. We could say, they have no intention of letting the facts get in the way of their reality.

I have found that for the student whose self-image is rigidly fixed, a particular demonstration may have to be repeated many, many times for them to change their point of view. In some circumstances, the teacher has to "remove the stablilizers" while the student is looking the other way, so to speak. For only then can the point be fully driven home, for only then can the student's reasoning processes be fully engaged with the reality of what has actually just taken place.

In my own case, my greatest difficulty in writing fiction in recent years has consisted more in embracing a new idea about myself, than it has in mastering the art and craft of story-telling. Surprising though it may seem, by far the biggest obstacle to my actually finishing a work of fiction has been a deep-seated conviction that "people like me" are not really writers, something I have been proving to myself for most of my adult life.

In the event, taking the time and trouble to actually finish a novel – and not caring too much if it was good or bad or indifferent – and subsequently acknowledging the accomplishment was a significant key to dismantling my fixed idea. Along the way, I had to keep reminding myself that once, long ago, stories came to me. As a young boy, I was always writing stories. Acknowledging this helped me to recognise that any absence of stories now, any lack of new and original ideas, was more likely the result of my shutting them out, than that I was story-less person.

In this process of changing the fixed idea I had of myself, I was giving myself the same lesson I give to my students. I asked myself to engage my reasoning processes with the facts of my

A great many students mistakenly believe that they can aid their chances of learning a new skill by employing a narrowing of the mind, which they refer to as concentration. All my teaching experience, however, suggests that this belief is a delusion. People invariably learn best when they stop "concentrating" in this way.

experience, and from there I came to the simple conclusion that writing fiction is one of my potentialities. It is something experience tells me I can do. Now I believe it. And belief is the biggest and most important step along the way.

As for writing well - ah, that's another story. To do that, I need to build on the foundation I am laying, only not according to my fixed, preconceived ideas.

Whenever we come across new ideas, for instance, the idea of stopping, then we must recognize that we bring to this idea an interpretation based on our current point of view.

"What is required is not prejudice in either direction, but a calm, clear, open-eyed intelligence, a ready, adaptive outlook, an outlook, believe me, which does not connote indefiniteness of purpose or uncertainty of intiative."

F M Alexander[10]

One student ("the psycho-analyst") will immediately construe this to mean that they must analyze their unconscious motives for interfering and then remove them; someone else ("the positive thinker") will look for a *stopping* state of mind and attend to replicating it whenever they can.

Each of these fixed approaches is likely borne of a desire to match a formula that has worked before to their current situation. However, neither of these approaches can be completely right, in that both - even if they lead to immediate improvements – will create their own limitations, and thus get in the way of the student gaining a control of all of their potentialities. In order to make ongoing improvements in everything we do, we need that flexibility in thought and action that is associated with reasoning and the free play of the imagination and therefore the absence of a fixed point of view.

In practice, one way we can loosen our attachment to our fixed ideas is to recognise alternative paradigms. For the person who is convinced that their idea of right is right and can conceive of no alternative is mentally rigid. Students who think in this way can only improve along the lines predetermined by their preconceptions. To really move forward, they must recover that flexibility of mind associated with multiple points of view, with an ability to engage with different and conflicting ideas.

History teaches us that the ultimate fate of those unable or unwilling to embrace new ideas is first to stagnate and then to perish. The world is changing. Our world is changing. We must change with it or be swept aside. In human affairs, in the art of living well, flexibility and success are wedded.

To conclude, let me say this.

We will be doing Alexander's work when we engage our minds with the task of changing our thinking to stop sending ourselves wrong. We will not do this by seeking to do the opposite of what we perceive to be wrong, nor by relying on our feelings to gauge progress, nor by sticking with our fixed, preconceived ideas. Instead, we will keep an open mind. We will remain open to new ways of building on the foundation we have laid.

We will go forward by working to let go of our fixed, preconceived ideas. For only when our paradigms are flexible can we continue to improve, for only then can we continue to make changes in ourselves.

"In human affairs, in the art of living well, flexibility and success are wedded."

Notes

1. pg 23, *The Seven Habits of Highly Effective People.*
2. pg 38, *Man's Supreme Inheritance*
3. pg 97, *Constructive Conscious Control of the Individual*
4. pg 29, *The Seven Habits of Highly Effective People.*
5. Please refer to: *If you want to be rich and happy, don't go to school.*
6. pg 9, *Freedom to Change.*
7. pg 96, *Constructive Conscious Control of the Individual.*
8. pg 172, *Constructive Conscious Control of the Individual.*
9. pg 63, *Man's Supreme Inheritance.*
10. pg 61, *Man's Supreme Inheritance.*

Checking the Compass to Chart the Course

It is incredibly easy to get caught up in an activity trap, in the busy-ness of life, to work harder and harder at climbing the ladder of success only to discover it's leaning against the wrong wall.

Stephen Covey

In the first three chapters we decided we would go to work on our thinking to stop generating an interference in the right working of ourselves in all our activites. The tool we would use is reason. In these chapters, I was primarily concerned with HOW we get ourselves to do what we do, in the precise sense of our *manner* of directing ourselves in activity.

If you succeed in working to these principles, you will change your way of going to work. You will sail your ship in a new and better way.

In the previous section, *Navigating Reefs and Rocks*, we looked at the ways people make ship-wreck, by failing to build on the foundation they have laid. In this section, we were still focussed on HOW, in the sense of our *manner* of directing ourselves in activity.

The next section is different, for chapter 7 is all about WHAT: chapter 7 is about the destination you seek, and the course you need to chart reach it. In this section, I will invite you to check the compass to chart the course; I will ask to re-commit to the destination you are headed, before going on to chart a course to reach it.

Seven
The Most Effective Way
taking simple, manageable steps

Question: 'How do you eat an elephant?'
Answer: 'One bite at a time.'"
- James Tolleson

At the beginning of our journey, I asked:

What is it you hope to achieve?

And to this question we will now return. I want you to re-examine and re-commit to the place you are headed.

"Even a blind squirrel will sometimes find a nut."

Don Weed

I said at the very beginning of our journey that aspirations do not have to remain fixed. It was true I needed you to pick a goal to get started, but your goal could always change in the light of new experience.

Sometimes, we have to actually set out on a journey before we get clear about exactly where it is we want to go, before we begin to realise the extent of what is possible for us. Nowhere is this more true than in Alexander's work. As people change the way they go about their business, they frequently find that the business they go about begins to change too. As we begin to stop creating distortions in the way we direct ourselves in activity, so our sense of who we are begins to shift. If we framed our early aspirations on the assumption that we were shaped like a square, we may want to change them if we discover we are more like a circle. As we let go of our preconceptions, so our aspirations may transform.

So: what is it you hope to achieve?

A failure to address this question, to keep addressing this question, can lead to a wasted journey. Too many people spend their lives climbing ladders, only to discover, as Stephen Covey writes, 'that it's leaning against the wrong wall.'[1]

Do you remember me in 1996, running a successful training and consultancy business? I was climbing higher and higher up a ladder, only deep down some part of me knew the ladder was no longer resting against the right wall for me. In this regard, we are all different. Each one of us is singularly unique. Given the choice, we would all pick a different destination. (As yet) no two people are exactly the same.

Sadly, too many people choose destinations that are incompatible with who they really are. One person spends their life chasing money, only to discover that the one thing which made them truly happy was painting. Someone else spends the bulk of their life pursuing painting, only to discover that painting was someone else's idea. All they really wanted out of life was intimacy.

As we get older, as we learn more about ourselves and our worlds, so our aspirations may change. We owe it to ourselves and to those who care about us to keep asking the question, for otherwise we run the risk of a wasted journey.

No one can decide for you what you want. Necessarily, you must decide this for yourselves. Certainly, the teacher can give you advice on the best way of choosing the place you want to go, but you will always have to decide. For example, for anyone unsure of what to do with their life, Robert Kiyosaki recommends using the thing they love most to do something about the thing they most hate.[2] He loves education and hates poverty, so he teaches people how not to be poor. It works for him.

In the field of drugs education, there are many differing ideas about what to do, some of them completely contradictory; for example, at one end of the spectrum attempts are made to scare young people from experimenting with drugs; at the other, young people are taught less dangerous ways of taking drugs. When I worked as a drugs educator in schools, I saw it as my job to inform teachers about the different approaches to drugs education and to help them to consider their respective advantages and drawbacks. Then I asked the teachers to identify strategies that would meet the needs of their particular school-children. As a rule, this narrowed down the field of possible options. Then I asked the teachers to select strategies that were consistent with their values. I asked the teachers: "What do you believe in?" Then I encouraged them to make choices consistent with values they shared.

"We can never hope to become all that we can be in matters about which we don't really care."

It was my view then – and still is - that teachers working away at projects they do not believe in is a recipe for failure. For anyone to become truly motivated, they must believe in their chosen destination. The place they are headed must connect to something true in themselves. This principle applies to drugs education, just as it does to any pursuit in life. We can never hope to become all that we can be in matters about which we don't really care.

So: if you come to my class and I ask you: "what do you want to work on?" my advice is to pick an activity that relates to something about which you truly care.

Time is precious. Your's and mine. So pick a goal about which you truly care.

That said, it is fine to be still unsure, to have only the faintest inkling. Just as it is equally fine to have such a clear vision that it burns a hole in your heart. All we are interested in here is getting better. We are seeking to identify and then apply principles that will enhance the quality of our lives.

*

We have a goal, and we are willing to change to achieve it. We will use our reasoning processes to change our thinking to stop interfering with the best direction of ourselves. In so doing, we will create the conditions necessary to give the right thing a chance to appear.

"Is that enough? I mean, enough to succeed? Or at least to improve?"

Yes. It often is.

"Often? So not always?"

No.

"Why not? I thought you said we were designed for success, so all we need to do is stop sending ourselves wrong. Didn't you say that?"

It's true we are designed for success. And I can't think of a better idea than going to work as if we were well-made. However, it's not always enough.

"Why not?"

Well, sometimes people lack good ideas.

"I thought we'd been over that in the last chapter. Now I'm confused."

Then let me explain.

I can't read music. I've never been taught and I've never tried to learn. If I am given a musical score and placed in front of a piano and asked to play a piece, I'm unlikely to succeed. No matter how well-co-ordinated I am; no matter how able I am to execute my ideas as I conceive them, it's not going to help. I have no idea what I need to do, what's involved in the task. You could say, I lack a correct conception of the act to be performed. When it comes to playing piano, that's something which is unfortunately true. When it comes to playing an étude by

Chopin, I have a lack of good ideas.

I am reminded of something that happened at school when I was nine or ten years old. I was summoned into the music-room. There, sitting at the piano, was a teacher I didn't know. She told me I was to be assessed, so that she could write my end-of-year report.

'Fine,' I said.

Then she struck a key on the piano. "Can you tell me what note that is?" she asked.

"What do you mean?"

She struck the note again. "What note is that?"

If you don't know what you need to know, you're extremely unlikely to succeed. Unless you get lucky. As we say in the ITM, even a blind squirrel will sometimes find a nut. No matter what the task, in almost every case, you need to be shown, or to figure it out for yourself.

I stared at her blankly.

Undeterred, she played the note again. "What *note* was *that?*"

"I don't understand."

She hit the key again. Surely she knew I'd never had a music lesson before.

"Give me a note, any note," she said, becoming impatient. (A queue of children were waiting outside.) I closed my eyes.

"A letter," she said. "Give me a letter. If you're not sure, have a guess. Come along."

"P."

"What?"

"P."

"Are you trying to be clever?" she said, standing up.

"No."

She sat down. She explained the letters went from A to G (without identifying them on the piano). She then played a number of notes. For each one I called out a letter from A to G. The test got done.

Perhaps, not surprisingly, my report card for music read,

"Anthony has difficulty in pitching notes."

There, I still remember. And to this day I have extreme difficulty in pitching notes. Basically, I can't sing in tune. Except that's not true. That would be a comfortable explanation for my difficulty. One in which my problem had nothing to do with me. As if I were tone-deaf, or something. Because, sometimes I do sing in tune. At least, that's what people trained to know tell me.

It may well be true that I don't hear pitch as well as others, but I do have evidence that some of my difficulty is in my mind. Otherwise, how do I explain that sometimes I pitch notes accurately? In fact, Chloe tells me that the incidence of my humming songs out of tune is becoming less and less. It would appear that, when it comes to singing in tune, as a consequence of going to work as if I were well-made, I am getting steadily better.

"Where the means-whereby are right for the purpose, desired ends will come."

F M Alexander

But, if we go back to the beginning, to me trying to guess notes for the music-teacher, it didn't matter what self-limiting ideas I did or did not have, nor did it matter if I had perfect pitch or was tone-deaf, I was not going to succeed. Unless, I got lucky. I didn't know the rules of the game she was playing. I lacked the information to play.

In teaching, what we sometimes encounter in students is a genuine lack of good ideas. They lack the information they need. Or, along the way, they picked up some wrong ideas. When this happens, no matter how successful they are in preventing themselves from sending themselves wrong, success, or even improvement, eludes them.

You see, if the student has lousy ideas, then improving how they get themselves to do what they do will simply mean they get better at realising their lousy ideas.

In the business of getting better, there is a place for good ideas.

So, in this chapter, I am claiming that, if you have an aspiration and you long to fulfill it, then, if you don't know how, you will have to figure out what it is you need to do. You will need to figure out the best course to take.

"So why wait till now, till chapter 7, before we re-examine what it is we want to achieve, and figure out the best course to take?"

Because what we find in teaching is that stopping the wrong thing is more often (but not always) where the biggest part of the student's problem lies. In life, about the things we truly care, often we have wonderful ideas. When this is so, if the teacher can just help the student to stop sending themselves wrong, then the student can be safely left to chart the best possible course for themselves. The student can figure out for themselves the steps they need to take.

Do you remember Vicky, Willie and Cynthia? They all had wonderful ideas about what they needed to do to achieve their goals. Vicky had identified a cognitive distortion; in her case, she needed to stop reacting as if it were true. As for Willie, he knew (knows) as much about the game of snooker as anyone; all he needed was to change the way he reacted to pressure so that he could demonstrate his mastery regardless of when and where. And Cynthia is a fine artist; she knows how to draw. Her problem was that she was creating unnecessary muscular tension; she was losing her ability to draw as she wished.

"If the mechanical principle employed is a correct one, every movement will be made with the minimum of effort."

F M Alexander

There are times, however, when, in the performance of certain tasks, it becomes clear that the student's conception of the act to be performed is so defective that improving the HOW will not get the job done at all. In situations such as these, we need to get the student to figure out what it is they need to do. They must reason out precisely WHAT they need to do. They must be encouraged to identify the steps they need to take.

*

In class, let us suppose that the student wants to work on a simple everyday activity, like walking, or going from sitting to standing, or typing on a keyboard at a desk.

According to how the student performs the chosen task, I might ask them:

"What do you need to do to [fill in the blank]?"

When I ask this question, I am looking to the student to give me their version of the WHAT, that is, the steps they need to take. In the ITM, we sometimes refer to this as the protocol. In terms of my voyage metaphor, it is the course we choose to chart (as opposed to our manner of sailing the ship).

When I ask the *what do you need to do* question, the answer I receive frequently suggests that the person has barely, if ever, consciously considered the most effective way of performing their chosen task. For example, let's suppose I ask: "What do you need to do to stand when you're sitting in a chair?"

Many beginning students will, if asked this question, look blank. They might even scratch their heads.

As it happens, I myself was just such a person. I'd never really thought about standing: I just stood. I went from sitting to standing *somehow;* I couldn't recall ever considering the steps I needed to take.

When I was first asked this question by my teacher, all I could come up with was driving my head upwards and somehow propelling the rest of me behind. I assumed the legs had to be involved, but I couldn't think how. In the event, when the teacher suggested a more effective protocol to me, it seemed so obvious I was puzzled that I had been unable to figure it out for myself. '*Why*' I wondered, 'could I not reason it out for myself?' At school, I had learned the basic principles of mechanics and I had studied the skeleton. But in practice, I was completely unable to link this knowledge up. When it came to the performance of everyday tasks, I behaved as if I were a complete mystery to myself. I acted as if I had no idea how I worked.

I have seen countless students struggle with these same, simple problems. They are so used to performing everyday tasks without thinking through what's involved, they are so used to performing routine acts in a fixed and mechanical way, that they are at a complete loss if asked to do otherwise. They have no idea where to begin. However, these same students will sometimes hold degrees in physics or engineering; these same students will be able to demonstrate an ability to test a scientific hypothesis, or even send a missile into space.

In my own case, the way I got myself to go from sitting to standing was remarkably consistent with the idea of driving my head upwards and pulling the rest of me behind. Instead of a simple, effective protocol, like bringing myself forward (by flexing at the hips) and then unfolding my legs, it seemed I was trying to turn on as many muscles as I could in my neck and torso, with some vague notion of propelling myself upwards like a rocket. Small wonder in everyday acts like standing up I employed large amounts of unnecessary muscular activity. Small wonder going from sitting to standing was not an activity I performed well.

For some students, an improved performance in everyday acts, whether it's standing, walking, or raising an arm, is of the utmost importance. Consider for a moment the painter whose arm and hand movements have become so stiff she can no longer work as a result; consider the dancer whose psycho-physical co-ordination has become so defective he can no longer learn new routines; consider the stage actor whose manner of performing everyday acts is crucial to portraying character.

When I first started having lessons, I did not see myself as one of these people: I was not especially interested in the performance of everyday acts. However, the principle of reasoning out the means, that is, figuring out the steps along the way, of selecting an effective protocol for reaching a goal, applies to each and every task. Whether I want to write a novel or slice a loaf of bread, whether I want to travel to California or wash the dishes, if I am to succeed, I must have an appropriate means in place. I cannot write a book just by stopping sending myself wrong; nor can I get to San Francisco by recovering my innate co-ordination. I will always need a plan, even if it's below the plane of my conscious awareness. On each and every journey, there will be a place for good ideas.

As it happens, it took me a very long time to realize that the thinking I employed in everyday acts, which was associated with a failure to reason out the steps I needed to take, was the same thinking I employed in more involved and exacting tasks. Whether I was going from sitting to standing, or sitting down to write a short story, I never once stopped to consider the appropriateness of the means I was adopting for achieving my goal. Just like F M in his reciting, I did whatever *felt natural.*

In practice, so long as I had effective protocols in place, everything worked out well enough. However, on those occasions when I did employ effective protocols, it was more by luck than design. I had, just like everyone I have ever known, developed the habit of doing whatever *felt natural,* of not thinking about what I needed to do. When it came to writing fiction, I used this same approach. On some days, this strategy worked really well; on others, the results were disastrous. Little did I know it then, but when I wrote badly, a significant part of my problem was my failure to clarify my intention and then reason out an appropriate strategy. As a consequence, on some occasions I gave expression to my good ideas; on others, I gave expression to the lousy ones.

In my early lessons, when I worked on everyday activities, I was being encouraged to begin the process of thinking differently. In this way, I was building a foundation for improvement, no matter what task I undertook. I was beginning to consider the appropriateness of my means for the end I had in mind.

These days, I frequently find myself asking questions like:

What do you need to do to write a good story?

Or:

What do you need to do teach an effective improvement class?

When faced with questions like these, I often think of Don Weed, who likes to quote James Tolleson by asking the following question:

"How do you eat an elephant?"[3]

Do not be fooled by the *how* at the beginning of the sentence. This question is, in the sense we have been discussing, all about *what*. We could translate it as:

"What do you need to do to eat an elephant?"

The answer, of course, is exactly the same way you'd eat anything: one mouthful at a time. This question serves to highlight the following principle: namely, that to succeed in any task, whether it is writing a book or slicing a loaf of bread, we will be helped if we break the activity down into simple, manageable steps.

And it is precisely here, in the process of breaking a chosen activity down into simple, manageable steps, that most students run aground. In practice, they either add steps in or miss steps out; or, if they get the steps right, they make them too big or too small. You could say, they eat the plate instead of the food, or they bite off more than they can chew. In some instances, a student will divide their meal up into such tiny portions, you might well imagine they could spend a life-time getting fed.

By way of an example, let's suppose a student wants to do something extremely simple like raising their arm. In the context of this particular principle, the question is: what do they need to do? In other words, we want to know what the most effective protocol is. We could ask: what are the steps they need to take? And further, what would count as a single, manageable step?

In his *Philosophical Investigations*, Ludwig Wittgenstein asks a similar question:

"What are the simple constituent parts of a chair? – The bits of wood of which it is made? Or the molecules, or the atoms?"[4]

Likewise, we might ask: "How many objects comprise a broom? Is a broom a single object; or is it two separate objects stuck together, that is, the broomstick and the brush? Or is all the many millions of molecules that make up the wooden handle and the individual brushes?"

The best answer to these seemingly impossible questions is, of course, that it depends on your point of view. If you are about to sweep up, then it's most likely one. If you are assembling brooms from sticks and brushes, then it's most likely two. If you are conducting a scientific experiment into the properties of different types of wood and plastic in the construction of brooms, probably a whole lot more.

The simpler we keep simple things, the easier it will be to make finer distinctions in more complex tasks.

Let us now return, with this idea in mind, to our first question, namely: what do you need to do to lift an arm?

In most cases that spring to mind, the best answer is: just lift it. If you want to raise your arm to attract the teacher's attention, just lifting your arm would be a simple, manageable step.

In this particular instance, there is no need to break the activity down into smaller steps. Contrary to the opinions of some, you do not need to know the precise location of the muscles involved, nor do you need to decide in advance the number of degrees of rotation, abduction and flexion of the humerus at the gleno-humeral joint. In most cases, just lifting the arm will be enough.

However, in a more complex task, like driving a car, we cannot hope to succeed if we do not have an appropriate means in place. To succeed, we must figure out or be shown what to do. We will have to work out the core, component steps. An effective protocol for driving will have to include looking out the window, steering, and the appropriate use of the accelerator, brake and clutch. If it doesn't, we won't get very far before we crash. It follows that, in all cases, no matter what we are trying to achieve, our protocol must be adequate to the task. It must include all the necessary steps.

In practice, however, we find that when students reflect on activities they perform regularly, they often struggle to figure out an appropriate means. To cite a common example, I once asked a student: "What do you need to do to play the cello?"

She replied that to the play the cello well she had to *make herself one* with the instrument. She then proceeded to show me. (In my view, this involved the creation of unnecessary muscular tension in her neck, torso and legs.)

"But what about the sound? What do you need to do to make a sound?" I asked.

She went quiet. "I don't understand the question," she said.

"What causes the sound?"

"Er..., you mean the bow moving across the strings?"

"Yes, and what do you need to do move the bow across the strings."

She went quiet again. At length, she said, "Move my arm?"

"Yes. That's right. Do you need to do anything else?"

She looked at her chest, her legs, and then her shoulders. "I don't think so."

"Then let's have another go, and this time see what happens if you simply move the bow across the strings."

In my view, she played much better.

For me, drawing the bow across the strings is a simple, manageable idea. In Alexander's work, we prefer simple, manageable steps.[5]

If you want to drive a car, you had better not leave out steering. If you want to play golf, you better not forget to strike the ball. If you want to sweep the floor, then you are making things needlessly difficult if your plan includes sorting out the precise angulation of the foot to the shin. By the same token, if you want to learn Alexander's technique, then you need to consider more than just the poise of your head.

No matter what our goal, no matter what we want to achieve, our means must be appropriate to our end. To succeed, we must always adopt an effective strategy. We can help ourselves in this task by breaking down tasks into simple, manageable steps. As Eintein says: "Everything should be made as simple as possible, but no simpler."[6]

"Everything should be made as simple as possible, but no simpler."

Albert Einstein

In summary: we will engage our minds with the task of changing our thinking to stop sending ourselves wrong in the performance of protocols we have reasoned out. To do this, we can make things easier for ourselves by taking simple, manageable steps.

Notes

1. pg 98, *The Seven Habits of Highly Effective People.*.
2. To be found in *If You Want to be Rich and Happy, Don't Go To School.*.
3. pg 22, *What You Think Is What You Get* by Dr Donald Weed.
4. paragraph 47, *Philosophical Investigations* by Ludwig Wittgenstein.
5. But what if the task is truly complex, like writing fiction? Surely, in that case, it would be a mistake to choose a simple means? If the task is complex, then surely we need a complex means?"

Well, let's pause for a moment to consider.

Let's suppose you really do want to do something truly involved, like writing a novel. And not just any old novel, but a really good one.

Now, on some level, in some way, if you are to work to this principle, then it is true that you must have an end in mind and select an appropriate means. However, that doesn't mean you have to decide in advance what you are going to write. You do not need to decide on the prose style, nor the plot, nor even the characters of the characters. What you do need, however, is a sense of what makes a good novel good. For the goal here, your aspiration, relates to the qualities you hope your book will embody. In this instance, what you need to figure out is what makes good fiction good.

Some writers can acquire this without ever formally identifying it. We could say they have developed an intuitive sense. However, when such a writer succeeds in writing well, then, on some level, we can infer that they do in fact have appropriate protocols in place, even if they would struggle to express them. If such a person came to my classes, I would in all likelihood only seek to draw their attention to the question of protocol if their writing suggested that there was a problem in this regard.

When the issue of what makes good fiction good is sufficiently resolved, you can begin to reason out the steps you need to take. You can begin to chart a course to your destination. And, according to your preference, you can do this before or during the process of writing. And what I am claiming here is that you will be helped in this if you succeed in keeping your protocols simple.

However, let's suppose that, in keeping with the idea of staying simple, you come up with a plan for writing a novel that only includes the ideas of plot, characterization, and consistency of narrative voice. In that case, I would have to confess that for me, as reader of such a book, the writing is unlikely to be sufficiently layered or rich. I might well be left asking: What about a theme? What about the imagery? What about the issue of how the prose style enhances or detracts from the central themes of the book? In reading fiction, these things interest me, and more things besides. They constitute my current idea of what makes a good novel good.

6. *Alles sollte so einfach wie moeglich gemacht werden, aber nicht einfacher.*

Sailing the Seven Seas

"Except for the point,
the still point,
There would be no dance,
and there is only the dance."

T S Eliot - The Four Quartets

In the final section we will encounter principles that will enable us to journey on towards our destination. We will discover the means for making our good ideas become real.

Eight

Mental Discipline

asserting your freedom to choose

"Suppose a man starts out to reach a certain destination and comes to a place where the road branches into two. Not knowing the way, he takes the wrong road of the two and gets lost. He asks the way of someone he meets and is told to go straight back to the crossroads and take the other road, which will lead him directly to the place he wants to reach. What should we say if we heard that the man had gone back to the crossroads as directed, but had there concluded that he knew better after all than his adviser, had taken again his old road, and again got lost, and had not done this once or twice, but over and over again? Still more, what should we say if we heard that he was worrying dreadfully because he kept getting lost, and seemed no nearer to getting to his destination?"

- F M Alexander[1]

We have come a long way. We have built a solid foundation. We have a sense of what we want to achieve and the steps necessary to achieve it. We have identified principles that will help us, and pitfalls standing in our way. But we are not home and dry. We are faced now with a choice: whether we go on as before, or branch out into the new. We have arrived at our very own fork in the road.

In lessons, following Alexander, I call the moment when we go from thinking about an activity into the actual performance of the activity the "critical moment." And it is to the critical moment I must speak now. This is the moment when Alexander is looking at himself in his mirror about to recite. This is when the student in a lesson is on the point of taking the first step. In fact, we can think of our lives as a series of critical moments: that is, opportunities to go on as you have always done or to step out into something new. The critical moment presents us with a choice, and the significant question is: in that moment, how able are you to assert your freedom to choose?

Following Don Weed, I call the ability to make that choice mental discipline. Mental discipline is your ability to choose. Specifically, mental discipline is your ability to choose against your habits of thought. To that extent, mental discipline is a potentiality we all have: it is a capacity with which we are all endowed. In experiential lessons, I help students to train this ability. When I work with students in the performance of everyday acts, I am seeking to give them reasons to choose against their habits of thought. And as they do this, so their mental discipline builds. It stengthens. With practice, students acquire an ever greater ability to direct their thinking according to their wishes. They reclaim their freedom to choose.

*

In class, when I begin to talk about mental discipline, a proportion of students will react badly. For some, the word "discipline" conjures up images of armies, or strict private schools, or a High Court Judge. For them, disicpline means life in the US Marines, or being taught by a Victorian school-master, or being punished by a patriachal Dad. For others, the word discipline has connotations of religious asceticism; it means fasting, ritualized prayer, or rising early everyday to meditate or go for a run. However, when I talk about mental discipline, that is not what I intend. No, my idea of mental discipline relates to your ability to sustain a certain freedom and flexibility in your thinking; in other words, to stay poised, open and fluid in your thoughts. The mental discipline I have in mind is not about so-called *will-*

power, rather, it relates to your ability to assert your freedom to choose.

So why do you use the word discipline?

Because discipline is still the best word. Only it is not the discipline that would deprive you of freedom, the discipline imposed from without. It is an inner discipline: it is your ability to direct your thinking as you wish.

With these ideas in mind, let us to return to Alexander's story. In particular, let's go back to that point early on in his journey when he figured out the best possible conditions for the use of his vocal mechanisms. You may remember that he found himself unable to put these new ideas into practice. He lacked the ability to work to the new procedure he had reasoned out.[2] As a consequence, Alexander was forced to consider the question of the direction of the use of himself. By what processes did he get himself to do what he did? How did he direct himself in activity?

F M tells us that he used himself habitually, that is, in whatever way *felt natural* to him. But this way was not working. In fact, this unreasoned way of going to work was the source of the problem, for it was precisely his habitual way of going to work that was associated with his hoarseness. The solution, you may remember, was to change his way of going to work, in particular to change the way he directed himself in activity. Instead of his instinctive, automatic direction of himself, he would employ a reasoning direction.

He writes:

> I came to see that to get a direction of my use which would *ensure* [this] satisfactory reaction, I must cease to rely upon the feeling associated with my instinctive direction, and in its place employ my reasoning processes, in order:

1. to analyse the conditions of use present;

2. to select (reason out) the means whereby a more satisfatory use could be brought about;

3. to project *consciously* the directions required for putting these means into effect.

In short, I concluded that if I were ever to be able to react satisfactorily to the stimulus to use my voice, I must replace my old instinctive (unreasoned) direction of myself by a new conscious (reasoned) direction.[3]

With this strategy in mind, F M went back to work. He decided to replace his old, instinctive direction of himself (which was associated with his pulling his head back and down), with a new, reasoned direction. In other words, he would employ his reasoning processes to change his thinking to stop sending himself wrong in the performance of a protocol he had reasoned out.

But then something truly surprising happened. F M found that he could not put this new, improved plan into practice either. To his amazement, he found that he could only employ a reasoning direction of himself up to the point just before going from planning into activity, but then, at the critical moment, just when he was about to speak the first words, he would revert to his old way of directing himself in activity. He would once again employ the thinking associated with his pulling his head back and down.

He writes:

"Over and over again I had the experience that immediately the stimulus to speak came to me, I invariably responded by doing something according to my old habitual use associated with the act of speaking."[4]

To his dismay, F M found that he lacked the ability to choose against his habit of thought. At the critical moment, he found himself unable to direct his thinking as he wished. Instead of following a procedure based on principles he had reasoned out,

"I must replace my old instinctive (unreasoned) direction of myself by a new conscious (reasoned) direction."

F M Alexander

he kept returning to the wrong, well-trodden path, associated with stiffness and hoarseness. To his dismay, F M lacked the mental discipline to sustain a new, reasoning direction through the critical moment and beyond.

As I write these words, I imagine any reader unfamiliar with Alexander's work lifting an eye-brow in surprise. "Surely that can't be!" they think. "Surely F M must have been unusual in not being able to carry out this plan. Surely, he must suffered from some mental defect, or have been an especially absent-minded fool!"

Let me assure you: Alexander was no absent-minded fool. On the contrary, he had cultivated and trained his mind. He had spent years studying the plays of Shakespeare and had undergone training in the dramatic arts. Yet, at the critical moment, he failed: he reverted to his habitual manner of use.

In practice, so ingrained was F M's manner of thinking in relation to the act of reciting that, regardless of his stated intention, regardless of his desire to work to the new principles he had reasoned out, he reverted to his habitual manner of use. In this, F M was like just about every student I have ever encountered. I know for a fact he was like me. Do you remember my first attempts at reading aloud stories I had penned myself? Well, in response to my anxiety, I turned myself into a performing disaster. In front of a live audience, I literally sabotaged my ability to perform. I was both surprised and embarrassed to discover I lacked the ability to direct myself in activity as I wished.

However, in my own case, I knew it hadn't always been so. I could remember a time when performing in front of an audience was a challenge I gladly accepted. I could remember a time when, long, long ago, I had the ability to direct myself on stage as I wished.

Let me tell you how this came about.

When I was only nine years old, I lived with my family in Surrey, just outside of London. I went to school with kids whose Dad's were milkmen, builders, gardeners, whose Mum's were shop assistants, hairdressers, cleaners. Basically, our parents did jobs for the stockbrokers and other professionals who lived in the big houses, who every morning dressed up smart to take the busy commuter trains to the City. As a consequence, my accent was strongly South London: like most of the people around me, I had little time for h's and t's.

At about this time, my Dad was becoming friends with one of the teachers at my primary school. He [the teacher] suggested I be sent for some elocution lessons to improve my speaking. My Dad was hoping I'd pass the exam to get into grammar school in a year or so, so it seemed like a good idea.

The elocution teacher they chose was an actress; and the method she adopted for teaching children was to get them to act. As a consequence, I was obliged to perform in front of other children. In the event, I enjoyed her classes immensely. The teacher soon had me and the other children taking acting exams. Within a year, I was travelling to London to take my Grade V Speech and Improvised Drama exam at Rada.

Once there, I had to recite some Shakespeare – which was a tall order, given the paucity of parts suitable for ten-year old boys – a poem, some prose, and last but not least, I had to improvise a short piece.

You may find this hard to believe, I know I do as I recall the experience, but this last bit was my favourite. There was nothing I enjoyed more than making things up on stage.

One of the examiners said: "I want you to imagine yourself in a strange place." She pointed to the centre of the stage. "You are lost. What happens next?" She looked at her watch. "Begin!"

These days, the very thought of being asked to improvise on stage, to make something up in the moment that will entertain an audience, stirs an anxiety within me. In response, I am tempted to abandon all the achievements of the last seven years and choose again the old, well-trodden path that leads down a hole of my own making. I am tempted to abandon my newfound freedom to choose. Tempted: yes.

But at the age of ten, improvising was my opportunity to

show the examiners what I could do. I surveyed my judges.
What did they want? To laugh? To be frightened? To be surprised?

I quickly came to a decision.

I needed to see a strange place: I looked around me and
there it was. Without pause, I set off down an imaginary road.
This was easy, because in some sense it was actually there. I had
to negotiate people, cars, a bus-stop, all the while contemplating
my foolishness at having taken the wrong bus earlier in the day.
I approached an old man sitting on a bench at a bus-stop. He
was fully fleshed out in my imagination: his clothes, his facial
expression, his demeanour. He was blind and carried a white
stick. He had a golden labrador by his side. I went over and
asked him where we were. But it turned out that the blind man
was lost too, in fact more lost than me. My improvisation was
about to take an unexpected turn. As I quizzed him, I discovered that he had no idea where he was. Worse, he no longer
cared. He was sad beyond measure. He had given up. I took it
upon myself to help him. All at once, I had to find out where
we were...

After, I hoped I had offered the judges something a little different to the wild panic in remote, exotic places I suspected most
of the other young actors would have portrayed. I tell you all
this to contrast this performance with my first attempts at reading on stage as an adult. For sadly, as far as I can recall, that was
the last improvised performance I ever gave. The next time I got
up on stage, more than twenty-five years later, to my dismay, I
discovered I was totally incompetent.

The day after my first performance as an adult, I had to ask
myself: what ever happened during the intervening years?
Where had I gone wrong?

One explanation that came to mind was that I had changed
my self-image; I no longer saw myself as a performer and therefore I lacked the ability to perform. However, although it was

doubtless true I had changed my ideas about myself, this explanation did not square too well with the fact that what I actually experienced was a seeming loss of psycho-physical co-ordination. On stage, it wasn't so much that I was thinking this isn't me and I can't do it; it was that I could no longer execute the ideas I had when I had rehearsed the piece at home. In the moment, I lost all sense of what I was trying to do.

Another explanation that occurred to me was that I lacked practice. However, I had in fact been practising relevant skills elsewhere for a number of years, for example, in speaking to large groups at conferences. The problem, as I experienced it, was my extreme response to my anxiety. In the heat of the moment, worrying about how what I had written would be received, I lost all contact with my reasoning mind; I was no longer able to direct my thinking as I wished.

The more I thought about it, the most convincing explanation for my poor performance as an adult was that I lacked the ability to direct my thinking according to my wishes, something I had found much easier in my early childhood years. As an adult, in response to my anxiety, I employed mechanical habits of thought associated with a deterioration in my general standard of performance. I quite simply abandoned my freedom to choose. As a ten-year old boy, I had not yet built up the proficiency in employing those incapacitating mental habits that characterized me as an adult: as a consequence, as a child, I was more able to stick with my good ideas.

"As a ten-year old boy, I had not yet built up the proficiency in employing those incapacitating mental habits that characterized me as an adult."

"Surely not?" I hear someone object. "As adults, don't we have much more mental discipline than children? Surely, as we get older, our mental discipline builds and builds?"

In most cases, in my experience, no, it does not; as we get older, we simply become more accomplished in recalling past protocols, that is, we come to develop an automatic proficiency in the performance of acts we routinely perform. However, that particular brand of proficiency, the kind that enables us to walk, to talk, to drive, to live the greater part of our lives without any so-called thought at all, is not what I intend when I refer to our ability to direct our thinking as we wish. No, the idea of mental discipline I wish to convey here is very different from the popular view..[5]

In this connection, I am reminded of a colleague who once told me that he had an Arnold Schwarzenegger mental discipline. His thinking was as hard as nails, he proudly said. His problem, however, was that every time he met a woman he fancied, he completely lost his head. He became so disoriented he couldn't speak a word. He told me he had come to the conclusion that trying to build his bulked-up discipline still further was a waste of time: it was his ideas about women that had to change. Now, doubtless it was true he needed to change his ideas about women, but I had to wonder about the thinking he was developing. At the critical moment, it certainly hadn't helped him to assert his freedom to choose.

So let me say this: if your current idea of mental discipline involves pumping iron, marching up and down in a straight line, or a relentless diet of water and brown rice, you've probably got the wrong idea. You might instead prefer to think of a group of children engaged in the act of playful make-believe, or of accomplished jazz musicians improvising together on piano, trumpet and sax.

But let's return to my story, to my problems reciting on stage.

Determined not to give up at the first hurdle, I talked to other performers and sought their advice. One highly successful performance poet told me that she always taped herself reading her pieces until she was confident she was reading them as best she could. Once she was happy with her reading, once she was clear in her own mind how the piece would sound to the audience, she acquired the necessary confidence on stage to perform at her best. For her, taping and listening was an important part of this process.

I duly went to a shop and bought myself a microphone. When everyone was out, I retreated to a bedroom with my tape-recorder to practise.

But to my dismay, I sensed myself tightening in my chest the moment I plugged the tape-machine in. I had felt a sudden twinge of anxiety, and my immediate response was to tighten muscles in my chest. Alas, just thinking about reading aloud, even in the privacy of my own home, seemed to be sufficient reason for me to change something in myself. Small wonder I had problems on stage!

I went and stood before a full-length mirror. I wanted to see if, like Alexander, I could identify any change in my response that I could work to prevent. I switched on the tape-machine, resolved to stay as calm as I could.

I didn't see myself pulling my head back and down as I had expected, but I definitely heard something. Just like Alexander, I noticed I gasped in a mouthful of air the moment I got ready to speak. At the same time, I felt a definite tightening in my throat. Whilst this was happening, I had the impression I was losing some of my clarity of thought. There was some kind of dizziness or vagueness clouding my thinking.

My first inclination was to *think harder*. I wanted to impose some clarity on my thoughts so that I could keep my mind on the job. However, I immediately recalled my lesson with John Gil, the one in which I had been unable to answer his question because he wouldn't allow me to do the thinking I believed I needed to do. I knew that thinking harder, or concentrating, at least as I conceived it then, was only likely to make matters worse. That was the thinking I habitually employed to make myself stiff.

What could I do?

The only other option I could conceive just then was to try to ignore my anxiety and just read the words off the page on some kind of automatic pilot. But when I tried this, I thought I read in a wooden, monotonous way. There seemed to be no feeling in my voice. This impression was confirmed when I played back the tape.

I began to feel truly stuck. I had come to a fork in the road. For some reason, I kept choosing the old, wrong path. It was time to change course, but I couldn't figure out how to do it. In the face of my own critical moment, it seemed I lacked the mental discipline to direct my thinking as I wished.

Alexander saw a need to: "make the experience of receiving a stimulus and refusing to do anything immediately in response."

*

F M Alexander never had any lessons designed to help him to build his mental discipline. Unlike me, he had to undertake all the work of changing himself in activity alone. Faced with the problem of sustaining a reasoning direction through the critical moment and beyond, he had to figure out his own solution.

F M Alexander tells us that, in order to escape from this impasse, he saw a need to:

"make the experience of receiving a stimulus and refusing to do anything immediately in response."[6]

In the ITM, and elsewhere, we call this practice *inhibition*. It is not inhibition in the sense of repressing thoughts or feelings, but rather inhibition in the sense of choosing against our habits of thought (expressed as habits of body), that is, of stopping sending ourselves down the old familiar pathway (expressed as our habitual manner of use). Inhibition, in this sense, is a specific mental discipline that can be practised to build up mental discipline in general.

In all likelihood, for the overwhelming majority of readers, the idea of inhibition presented by Alexander here is new. Therefore, I would like to say a few words to clarify some common misunderstandings.

Firstly, lets take a look at "make the experience." Many readers are tempted to gloss over these opening words. In so doing, however, they miss the point that inhibition is a *volitional* (psycho-physical) activity. It doesn't happen of its own accord. You have to make it happen. You have to create the experience for yourself. To that extent, inhibition is a choice. You either carry on as before, or you branch out into the new.

Second, let's take a look at precisely what it is we are going to make the experience of.

Alexander is clear on this: it is the experience of *receiving a stimulus and refusing to do anything immediately in response.* In other words, inhibition is the self-created experience of refusing to do anything immediately in response to a given stimulus. F M is saying that he saw a need to bring together *receiving* and *refusing to do* into a single, self-generated experience.

Recently, I was reading an exchange about the Alexander Technique on the internet. One of the contributors claimed that inhibition was the experience of *recognizing* a stimulus and refusing to anything immediately in response. This slight shift in reading turns the emphasis of inhibition away from mental discipline towards sensitivity or awareness training. However, Alexander wrote *receiving a stimulus.* Why? What does he mean? Surely, in one sense, we are receiving stimuli all the time. Isn't everything we experience a stimulus?

The first thing to say is that what counts as a stimulus in any given circumstance does in fact depend on your point of view. Do you remember Wittgenstein's broomstick? We asked: How many objects comprise a broom? It depended, of course, on our point of view. Likewise for stimulus. However, in the specific context of practising inhibition, we can be more precise. For Alexander is concerned with stimuli that tempt us (give us reason) to choose our habitual manner of directing ourselves in activity. In his case, the desire to recite was an approriate stimulus. In mine, the idea of reading my own fiction to a live audience. In Vicky's case, if you remember, wanting to sell a painting. In Willie's, preparing to pot a ball to win a major championship. In Cynthia's, trying to draw freely. To that extent, any desire to act will likely prove to be an adequate stimulus for the purpose of practising inhibition. Any stimulus that is associated with our unthinking adoption of fixed habits of thought in the performance of a particular activity.

We could pick the desire to sit, to stand, to write, or even to look cool in front of our peers. We could focus on any idea that we routinely respond to according to our fixed habits of thought associated with our habitual manner of directing ourselves in activity. It is up to us to decide.

Next, what does Alexander mean by *refusing to do anything immediately*?

Some people, I have heard it reported, have thought Alexander meant by this doing nothing, in the sense of sitting or standing still. These people convince themselves that they are practising inhibition if they sit quietly on a chair, or lie down motionless on the floor, and think about getting up. But that is not what Alexander meant.

For when Alexander writes *to do* here, he means doing in the sense of our habitual doing. The stopping he is interested in is the refusal to walk down the old familiar pathway in response to the receipt of a stimulus. Whether or not the person stays still has no bearing on this fact, for the student can in fact choose not to move by employing their fixed habits of thought. Clearly, we do not want this. On the contrary, we want the student *to do nothing* by *refusing* to generate their habitual misdirection. We want them to refrain from rushing headlong down the old wrong pathway. In other words, we want them to stay in communication with their reason. We want them, for example, to continue organising their thinking according to principles they have reasoned out.*

To that extent, I can practise inhibition by making the decision not to respond habitually to the thought of reciting my work in public. All I need to do to do this is to stay in communication with my reason. It is a simple choice I can make. And, as I practise making that choice, so my ability to make that choice builds.

I can stand in front of the mirror and think about reading my work aloud. Whether or not I do so is irrelevant. The key is whether or not, in response to my desire to perform, I sustain my new, reasoning direction of myself, or abandon it in favour of my old, habitual response.

To summarize: in response to the stimulus of wanting to recite, I can practise making the experience of refusing to do anything immediately. By practising the specific mental discipline of inhibition, so my mental discipline in general builds.[7]

*

In the classes I teach, the principle of mental discipline crops up in practically every lesson.

In this connection, I recall that some months ago I happened to be giving Cynthia a lesson. You may recall, Cynthia

---

*   It has been objected that F M really does mean *doing nothing at all* when he writes *refusing to do anything* immediately. However, on some level, we are always involved in some kind of activity, even if only sitting or standing, and to that extent it is commencing a new activity that matters. In view of this, I can, for example, practice inhibition in relation to a desire to raise my arm even if I am walking down the street. The all-important issue here is not employing my fixed habits of thought in relation to the stimulus to some new or extra activity.

wanted a certain freedom and ease of line in her drawing. However, when she attempted to stay free, she tightened worse than ever.

I began by going over the ground we had covered in the previous lesson. I reminded Cynthia that she had no need to concentrate (as she conceived it) to draw well. Cynthia agreed. She told me she recognised the folly of trying to stay free in her body (as she conceived trying), as she had been doing before. She told me she had given up that false idea.

"Wonderful," I said. "Would you like to draw today?"

"Yes," she said.

In the event, Cynthia began well enough. She drew easily and with confidence, but then, after only the first few lines of her sketch, she began to stiffen her fingers, arm and hand. She sensed the change in herself and stopped.

"Why did I go stiff?" she asked me. "I wasn't trying to stay free that time. It just happened."

"It would easier for me to show you than to explain in words," I said. "Would you like to draw some more?"

I got Cynthia to draw again. This time I placed my hands on her in such a way that it was much easier for her not to generate her habitual misdirection. As a result, she was able to sustain her original direction long into the drawing. When I sensed the time was right, I removed my hands. Cynthia carried on drawing without the usual stiffness creeping back.

"Same or different?" I asked.

"Different. Better."

"What was different?"

"Something was missing. It felt a lot easier, as if I was doing less."

"So what did you change?"

"I don't know, my thinking, I guess."

"That's right, your thinking."

"But I could only do it with your hands on me. I couldn't do it alone."

"But you did. My hands were over here at the end."

"I know, but you got me started. How does that work?"

"Let me put it like this. The impetus you set off with was good. My hands simply served to remind you not to forget it."

"Will I be able to do it again next time by myself."

"Yes. All you need to do is remember. And each time you make that decision it becomes easier. Bit by bit, you are building your freedom to choose."

And as Cynthia makes that decision, so her drawing gets better. She finds again the freedom and ease of line she thought she had lost. She reclaims her freedom to choose.

In lessons, if I can work with a student in such a way that they carry out an activity without their customary misdirection, I can help them to break down their habit of thought. This not only builds their confidence in their ability to think differently, but helps the student generate an experience for themselves of employing a manner of thinking better suited to their purpose. Insofar as they are able to correctly apprehend this new experience, so it becomes easier for them to choose this manner of thinking again. I am showing the student how easy it is for them to think differently; you could say, I give them a demonstration of their freedom to choose.

"But why would Cynthia, or you, or anyone for that matter, adopt habits of thought that undermine their ability to perform? It just doesn't make sense."

The particular reasons we have for interfering with ourselves are plenty and varied: for example, imitation of family members, to cope with uncomfortable feelings, to deaden physical pain, to create a particular impression for significant others.

In my own case, after much reflection, I was led to conclude that I had spent a good deal of the last twenty-something years training myself to hide my nervousness in public. And the method I had chosen was simple. I created or adopted a fixed attitude of mind. Metaphorically speaking, I made sure there was no wobble in me for others to see. In so doing, I literally threw away my ability to think creatively; I abandoned my freedom to choose.

Some might be tempted to call the training I had subjected myself to self-discipline, in the sense of the discipline required to maintain a stiff upper lip; however, this is the antithesis of what we are looking for when we talk about mental discipline in Alexander's work. For if we pursue that kind of training, of making ourselves rigid in response to anxiety, we run the risk of ending up so frozen as to be incapable of an intelligent (and hence, by extension, emotional) response.

Doubtless I and many others had good reason as children to so train ourselves, for example, the merciless bullying we presumed we would be subjected to if anyone got wind of the fact we were scared. Good reason, yes: justification, surely. But not, I say with some hope, a necessary and sufficient cause. We can always change our minds. We can always choose against our habits of thought.

In practice, evidence of my relative success or failure in inhibiting my habitual response can be found, paradoxically, in my movement behaviour. For when I succeed in choosing against my habits of thought in response to the idea of performing on stage, there is an absence of my habitual tightening in my neck and chest. When I sustain a reasoning direction of myself through the critical moment and beyond, I perform at a higher standard. In order to be able to think in this way, on demand, regardless of the circumstances, I can help myself by practising the mental discipline of inhibition. I can do this now, when writing, or when rehearsing, or when teaching, or when I go about my daily business. The more I practise, the easier it becomes to choose against my habits of thought.

I am pleased to report that the principle of mental discipline provided me with a way out of the impasse created by my inability to stick with a protocol I had reasoned out for reciting on stage. Little by little, I broke down my habit of abandoning my reasoning processes in response to my anxiety. Little by little, the readings I gave improved. Which is not to say that reading aloud stories I have penned myself does not present a challenge to me. It does. Likewise, reading aloud is a task I can easily imagine performing at a much higher standard than I currently do, but it is an activity at which my standard of performance is improving. In fact, my general standard of performance in all my activites gets better as my mental discipline builds.

I am still some way short of attaining the ability to direct my thinking I enjoyed as a child, but I am steadily improving. Year by year, I am confident my general standard is getting better. And that's what matters. All we are interested in is getting better. The tools in this book are designed to help you to improve.

In conclusion, let me say this: to reach our goal, to fulfill our aspiration, we will endeavour to employ a reasoning direction of ourselves in the performance of a protocol appropriate to our task. We will cultivate the mental discipline necessary to move through the critical moment and beyond. We will assert our freedom to choose.

Notes

1. pg 103, Constructive Control of the Individual.
2. pg 31, *The Use of the Self*.
3. pg 39, *The Use of the Self*.
4. pg 40, *The Use of the Self*.
5. An issue that troubles many students in this regard is why adults are in fact able to perform at a much higher standard than children in a great many activities. If, as I am claiming, children on the whole enjoy a greater flexibility in their thinking, as a consequence of not employing fixed habits of thought to the same extent as the majority of adults, then why do they not do as well as adults in a great many tasks? The solution to this particular paradox is simply that children lack experience; in practice, they are less likely to have appropriate protocols in place, for they have spent a lot less time figuring out, or being shown, what's involved in a particular task. I am not claiming, however, that we should seek to make ourselves like children again, that we should look for a pathway backwards. On the contrary, we seek to reclaim the lost flexibility in our thinking by learning how to discipline our minds. In this, we are going forwards.
6. pg 40, *The Use of the Self*.
7. From time to time, a student will ask: "Is inhibition the only discipline Alexander practised?"

No, there were in fact others.

But in an introductory how-to book based on an introductory how-to course, there is no justification for mentioning more. In fact, many teachers would argue that by mentioning inhibition I have already introduced too much advanced material. However, if you have studied the material in the previous chapters, and you are mindful not to read this chapter according to your fixed, preconceived ideas, I think you are ready. If, however, you want to know more, then you should read chapters 9 through to 13 of *What You Think Is What You Get*, which is based on (at least in part) the final section of the first chapter of *The Use of the Self*.

The next question, of course, is: "Does this mean that without the other specific disiplines F M practised I will be unable to practise his technique?"

No. Certainly not.

If you succeed in working to the principle of mental discipline based on the practice of inhibition, you will create the conditions for profound and significant change throughout your life. You will create the conditions for going forward. Let me assure you: you will create the conditions for far-reaching and lasting improvement in everything you do.

Nine

Genuine Trust

stepping into the unknown

"Jump and the net will appear." – Julia Cameron

"Everything a person has done in the past has been in accordance with the mental direction to which he is accustomed, and it is his faith in this that makes him unwilling to exchange it for the new direction one is trying to give him." - F M Alexander[1]

"Mr Alexander's work is reasoning from the known to the unknown..."

Joseph Rowntree[2]

We have a sense of where we are headed, and the steps we need to take to move on. We have taken the first steps down a new and different pathway. It is now, in this moment of transformation, that we encounter one of the most serious obstacles to progress, and that is the experience of *feeling wrong*. Yes, as we leave our old ways behind, as we take the right path at the crossroads, we are confronted with a new experience of ourselves. For many, this new experience is akin to walking into a strange and unfamiliar land. As a consequence, from somewhere deep inside a voice may well scream out: "No, this is wrong!" In spite of this, we must find the courage to hold our course, the conviction necessary to press on. In the moment of transformation, we must trust in the path we have chosen.

*

Just the other day, Leif learned to ride his bike. One of his stabilizers had fallen off, and so his friend, Henry, had shown him how to ride without them. The key to success, according to his six-year-old mentor, was in getting going. If you point the bike straight ahead, and then drag your foot along the ground, so that you propel yourself forward, then you can find your balance before beginning to pedal. Once you are going, you just add pedalling in.

Leif gave it a go. He pushed himself off, and once he realized he was in fact balancing without the stabilizers, he just added pedalling in. Now he rides with confidence.

Did it help that Henry was only a few months older than Leif, that Henry was able to demonstrate riding the same bike without stabilizers himself? I don't know. But what I do know is that learning to ride for Leif (as for everyone) required trust. For once he pushed himself off, there inevitably came a moment when he rolled to one side and didn't get the feeling of the stabilizers touching the ground. In response, he could have lurched the other way to counter the feeling of falling and thus really lost his balance, as most people do when learning to ride a bike without stabilizers, or he could trust in the new protocol suggested by his friend and so make a small adjustment of the front wheel to continue in the direction he wanted to go. In the event, this latter course was the choice he made. He chose not to react instinctively to the feeling of falling, and instead stuck with the new protocol for riding instead.

Now when Leif rides his bike, the feeling of falling is not a sensation he has to eradicate at all costs; it is simply information that he can use to help him to maintain his balance.

I tell you this story to highlight a key principle in Alexander's work, namely trust, or genuine trust. For to carry on further along our chosen path, we must cultivate a genuine trust in the principles we have reasoned out, that is, a trust that will enable us to carry on irrespective of what or how we feel. For when we make a change in ourselves, when we stop directing ourselves in activity as we have always done, in almost every case, what we experience will be unfamiliar and strange. More often than not, the experience will be good, wonderful even, but not always.

The only thing we can be reasonably sure of is that we will have a new experience of ourselves. In this, we will be stepping into the unknown. And to do this, we need genuine trust in the path we are taking, for the "lure of the familiar" is strong, and we often balk at the prospect of experiencing what is new or strange.[3]

*

In chapter 5, you may remember, we talked about *feelings* primarily in the sense of interpretation of sensory data. We noted, however, that there were other meanings of the word, for example, direct sensory input, as in, "I feel pain," and also emotion, as in, "I feel sad." In this chapter, we need to keep in mind these other meanings of the word, for we are interested in the wider notion of feeling when it represents experience in general.

In this chapter, we will be especially interested in the experiences students have of themselves when they stop going about their business in their usual way. We will consider the issue of what students feel when they leave behind what is familiar and known; we will consider the wide range of experiences students tend to characterize as *feeling wrong*. This is important, for students will often react to feeling wrong by charging back to the cross-roads and taking the old wrong path once more.

The experience of *feeling wrong* shows up repeatedly in lessons, and nowhere more so than in activities that involve walking, for the simple reason that students have grown so accustomed to their particular way of moving on their legs, that to make a constructive change often generates the feeling of loss of balance. In the face of this feeling, a great many students will baulk. In practice, they demonstrate a preference for what is familiar, or *feeling right*, over and above improvement.

As a fairly typical example, one of my students, Philip, has an unusual way of standing that involves thrusting his head and pelvis forward, at the same time locking his ankles, knees and

hips. When I work with him to prevent these self-generated movement behaviours, he has a new experience of himself, which, though unfamiliar, he finds reasonably enjoyable. He has the impression of standing with a great deal less effort. So far so good.

When, however, I ask him to take a step forward to commence walking, we run into serious trouble. Not so much because he lacks the mental discipline to sustain this new way of thinking through the critical moment and beyond, but because, as soon as he moves a leg, he doesn't get the usual sensory feedback he has come to associate with walking. It feels so wrong, he is convinced he will fall over, and so he plunges his moving leg into the ground, in a desperate bid to reclaim the lost feeling, which he equates with standing up. Philip quickly comes to a grinding halt.

In taking that first step, Philip is just like Leif on his bike without stabilizers for the very first time. In the absence of the usual feeling, he is convinced he will fall, and so his main concern is to eradicate the feeling, as opposed to carrying on with the new protocol he has reasoned out.

In recent weeks, however, Philip has made great progress, which has required a remarkable degree of trust; and for his success in this he is owed tremendous credit. For Philip has had to learn to trust in a new way of directing himself in activity, which is not accompanied by his familiar feelings, upon which he has grown to depend. To make progress, he has had to stop listening to a loud inner voice screaming, "No, this is wrong!" He has to listen to the voice of reason instead.

In writing about Philip, I am reminded of an experience I had myself, only not during a lesson but a few days later.

Many years ago, I guess about six months after I had begun studying Alexander's technique, I went into my local coffee shop early one morning to buy a coffee. (On this particular day, I had not as yet spoken to anyone.) The moment I opened my mouth, however, I knew something was wrong, seriously wrong. For instead of my usual weak, faltering whisper, out came a deep, resonant command. I was shocked, so much so I almost choked on my words. Within seconds, I found myself recreating the usual tension in my throat, so that my voice returned to it's sickly self. In this, I got back my usual feeling in speaking, and some part of me breathed a huge sigh of relief.

If I attempt to analyze what happened that morning in the coffee-shop, it seems I had simply forgotten to create the usual tension in my throat, associated with my habitual way of speaking, as a consequence of learning Alexander's technique. Unfortunately, the new experience of speaking felt so wrong to me, in the sense of so alien, I quickly leapt back to more familiar ground. Doubtless I was speaking better, but it just didn't feel right. In fact, it felt horribly wrong. In changing the way I directed myself in activity, I was quite literally losing my everyday sense of my speaking self.

I have seen this same phenomenon happen to a great many students when working on activities they habitually perform.

Typically, musicians act as if they believed that a certain feeling of tension in various parts of their body is necessary for playing their particular instrument. Without it, they struggle to believe they can play, or at the very least play well. For example, singers and brass-players frequently create inordinate amounts of tension in their necks, which in practice only serves to restrict the sound they make as opposed to amplifying it. However, if I work with them in such a way that they stop needlessly tightening in their throats, many will balk at the idea of playing or singing altogether. For in this improved condition they lack the feeling of tension they have come to associate with performing at their usual standard. As a consequence, they fear the sound they will make would be too weak, assuming, that is, they believe they can make any sound at all. However, if they can be persuaded to sing or play and maintain these improved conditions, the rest of the group almost always report an improvement in the quality and quantity of sound, sometimes to the dismay of the performer. Sometimes, the experience of performing in this new way feels so wrong, the musician will persuade themselves that the sound is worse. "I was too quiet," they will complain. "No, you were louder," report the group. "I was all over the place," the performer will say. "No, that time the sound was vibrant and free."

Of course, I sympathize with these performers completely, for I have had a similar experience myself when reciting on stage.

I have, on more occasions than I care to recall, practised reading a piece at home in front of the mirror until I was satisfied that I was reading it well, only to find that, the moment I got up to read on stage, I filled with anxiety. Then, as we discussed in the last chapter, I needed an adequate mental discipline to maintain the improved conditions for reciting. However, the extent to which I succeeded in employing this new discipline, something seemingly far worse happened: I had a new experience of myself, that is, I heard myself reading aloud well while at the same time feeling completely fearful. To me, that *felt wrong*. In that moment, all I craved was to feel right, in the sense of having a more familiar experience of myself.

"His very desire to 'be right in gaining his end' defeated the end."

F M Alexander

For me, it used to (and still does on occasion) feel so *wrong* to be reading clearly and well, when my heart is pounding and my legs are shaking, I have trouble believing I can carry on. I find the experience quite disturbing. When this happens, all I want is to return to more familiar ground. And the easiest way for me to do this is to recreate my old way of directing myself in activity, associated with unnecessary muscular tension. If I simply tighten the muscles in my neck, torso and legs, I instantly get back to a place I know well. For when nervous, that is what I have learned to do. In fact, it is one of the things in the course of my life I have practised most diligently. However, some part of me knows that to give in to this temptation would be to jettison the improved approach to reciting I have reasoned out, as I would almost certainly create an interference in the right working of my head in relation to my body, which is associated with a deterioration in my general standard of performance.

Here then is the choice I face: I can feel right, or continue with the new thinking I have reasoned out is best suited to the task. I can't do both. In that moment, when I hear myself reading well, without the usual tension in my throat, chest and legs, to continue *feels wrong*. And let me assure you, feeling wrong in reciting is far worse than the feeling of nervousness I have when getting up on stage, for it involves carrying on without the only response to anxiety I have practically ever known. I am called upon to give up my old sense of self. I really do have to step into a strange and unfamiliar land. And right then, in that moment of transformation, if I am to carry on further down my chosen path, what I need is trust. I need to trust that the new approach to reading aloud out will see me right. I need to trust in the new direction (to which my reasoning processes are pointing), irrespective of what or how I feel.

As F M Alexander wrote in *The Use of the Self*:

"My trust in my reasoning processes must be a genuine trust, not a half-trust needing the assurance of feeling right as well."[4]

For so long as I cling to my desire to feel right, I will stick with my old way of going to work. I will return to the crossroads and take the old wrong path once more.

"My trust in my reasoning processes must be a genuine trust, not a half-trust needing the assurance of feeling right as well."

F M Alexander

*

In Chapter 5, we considered the relationship between feelings and ideas and concluded that feelings (at least in the sense of interpretation of sensory data) are fashioned by ideas. To that extent, what any one person will feel when they make a constructive change is largely unpredictable, as each and every person has their own unique set of beliefs. However, in teaching, we often see a relationship between the new experience a student has of themselves when they make a constructive change and the assumed problem for which the unnecessary muscular tension was originally (or still is) a solution.

You may remember Sid, who experienced a dull ache in his shoulder every time he interfered less. For me, this is evidence to suggest that the increased tension served at least in part to obscure the pain in his shoulder, for the simple reason that, whenever the pain comes, he is tempted to tighten more. (This type of occurance, when a student feels an increase in discomfort upon making an improvement, although disconcerting, is not so rare, particularly in situations where the distorting movement behaviour successfully masks feelings associated with past physical injuries. I do not as yet know whether this is the case for Sid.)

Sometimes, however, the changes in feeling happen more indirectly, and not with regard to a specific activity, or during the lesson itself. Let us consider the case of Stephen.

Stephen came to my introductory course, and initially loved the changes he made. He felt more connected to himself, in less physical pain, and with a renewed sense of the possibilities of his own life. However, as the course progressed, he came to feel ever more empty and sad.

Stephen was concerned to be feeling this way. It didn't seem right. He was wondered if Alexander's work was the cause of these feelings. However, as we approached the end of the course, it became clear to him that part of the purpose of the unnecessary tension in himself that he was leaving behind was to mask his true feelings. For each time he made a change, irrespective of how empty he felt, he remembered that he always said, "This feels more real."

Stephen discovered that there was indeed an emptiness in his life, which he somehow managed to avoid facing up to by creating distortions in himself associated with pulling his head back and down. As he stopped interfering with the poise of his head in relation to his body, so he experienced himself more fully. He came to see that it was time to move on with his life: he was ready to re-connect with other people. He wanted to be intimate again.

I, myself, when I had my early lessons with John Gil, had a

similar experience. Initially, I felt a certain lightness, a feeling of pleasure in activity, a renewed enjoyment in everyday physical acts, like walking, lifting, stretching. However, the more lessons I had, the more bored I became with my life, especially the administrative side of running a business, which was taking up seemingly vast amounts of my time. I began to feel more and more irritated with the balance of my working days. I took an aversion to doing cashflow forecasts, to drawing up contracts for clients, and writing reports on work already accomplished. Previously, I had just knuckled down and got the work done.

Unlike Stephen, I didn't wonder if the Alexander work was the cause of my distress, I was sure it was. I complained to John, and told him I was feeling increasingly irritated or bored. My world was losing all its richness, I said. As a consequence of doing Alexander's work, I was living in a black-and-white world - I wanted the colour back!

In response, John told me a story about a round peg trying to live in a square hole, and the uncomfortable feelings the poor round peg had. At the end of the lesson, he asked me consider whether I felt irritated and bored simply because I was.

Over time, I came to the painful realisation that one of the purposes of the unnecessary muscular tension I was creating in myself was to mask my true feelings. Sure enough, as I began to listen to these feelings, which arose in conjunction with my doing less, the balance of my life began to change. And change for the better. In no time at all, I made the decision to give up working as a full-time manager. Deep down, I had known for a long time that the direction Gil was taking was no longer right for me, and that I had to start writing fiction again.

In this connection, I am reminded of an incident that occurred when I worked as a young people's counsellor at a drug and alcohol advisory service. On this particular day, I was booked to see someone who was 25 years old, right at the top end of my age-range; I must have been about the same age myself.

The young man in question walked into my office. He was

in a very distressed state, unable to look at me or sit still in his chair. I asked him why he had come. He told me he had been drinking for 10 years. Not a day had gone by that he could recall since he was 15 years old when he hadn't got drunk. He had to stop now. He was losing everything, his job, his girlfriend, his home. Ever since that first drink, he had been on a bender. If he didn't stop, he'd kill himself, or someone else.

Inexperienced as I was, it was my job to refer him for appropriate treatment, for example, AA, counselling, "detox.", or a support group, or even to offer to meet with him myself. A certain amount of information gathering was in order.

"Did anything happen 10 years ago to start you drinking?" I asked.

"No."

"You had one drink and then you couldn't stop? And haven't stopped since?"

"That's right."

"You were only fifteen at the time… so were you living at home?"

"No, I started drinking immediately after I left home, within a few days."

"Was there a reason for leaving home? I mean, you were only fifteen?"

"Well, my Dad died, and so there was no point staying. I just packed a bag and left."

"And you started drinking within a few days and haven't stopped since?"

"Yeah."

"And, as far as you are concerned, the two events, your Dad dying and starting a 10 year bender, are unrelated?"

He was about to reply when he stopped. He looked up from the floor for the first time and met my gaze. He stared at me. He didn't look away. It was if he wanted me to answer the question arising for the first time inside him. Slowly his face took on a look of anguished disbelief. Alarm-bells were ringing in his head; a light had suddenly been switched on. "You're not saying

…?" He slumped back in his chair. "My Dad died and… and I've been drinking ever since."

I looked at him as neutrally as I could.

"Unbelievable," he said at last. "It's so obvious, it can't be true."

Within minutes, he was overcome by grief.

Now, I do not know whether or not the two events were related. There are many theories of alcoholism, and for that reason alone it would be rash to claim they were. However, this young man made a connection in his own mind. Significantly, all the feelings were still there within him. In his case, he came to believe he had drowned them out with booze.

In teaching my improvement classes, I have seen a similar process at work. When working with people to help them undo their unnecessary doing, I have sometimes seen a similar phenomenon. For a number of students, the moment they desist from a particular way of directing themselves in activity, a buried feeling will on occasion come to the surface. For that reason, sometimes making progress can feel *wrong*, (and not just feeling in the sense of interpretation of sensory data), even if the feelings (emotions) the student experiences are genuine, even if, what is more, they have no basis in the students life as it is now. For some people, the welling up of past memories with associated feelings in a lesson is disturbing, yet it may be a quite normal response to a diminished interference in themselves, especially if the original impetus for interfering was to rid themselves of memories or feelings they didn't like.

As an example of this, let us review the case of Vicky, who suffered, you may remember, from a cognitive distortion regarding positive comments she received from others regarding her work. In Vicky's case, when I worked with her in lessons, the biggest constructive changes were always associated with the emergence of feelings and impressions which left her feeling uncomfortable, for they ran into direct conflict with her distorted view of herself.

In Vicky's case, significant diminishments in the distortion in the relationship of her head to neck, and her head to neck and torso, always resulted in her standing taller and looking more confident, and, to my mind, more self-possessed and attractive. However, in the early days, instead of enjoying this new condition, Vicky was quick to reject it. She didn't like the change: it *felt wrong* to her. And the reason it felt wrong was that the change deprived Vicky of her usual sense of self, which, although not ideal, she at least found reassuring.

Initially, Vicky would claim that if she walked down the street in this changed condition, she would draw attention to herself in a number of quite different negative ways. Onlookers would either see someone arrogant and vain, or so vulnerable they would be an obvious victim, or someone keen to invite the sexual interest of any passing man. On occasion, I probed her on this, and she told me that her new impression of how she appeared to others was accompanied by memories from her childhood of incidents almost too painful to recall.

The "improved" condition *felt wrong* to Vicky, so wrong, in fact, that she longed to revert to her former self. However, there was something about the changed condition she liked, for when she made this change in herself, not only did she feel freer and less stiff, but she could register that she was breathing more easily.

What is more, the feedback Vicky received from others in the group when I worked with her was singularly positive. People would say: "Now you look, calm, confident and poised. I prefer you like this."

"I'm sure I don't," Vicky would protest.

Over time, it became clear to Vicky that she would have to either to trust the feedback she was getting from others, or continue to trust her own sense of self. She couldn't do both.

In the event, as the lessons progressed, Vicky began to trust in the more objective assessment of the teacher and the group, and less in her subjective sense of self, based as it was on her interpretation of her feelings.

Step by step, Vicky began to accept that her sense of how she appeared to others was more than likely wrong, and as a consequence of this changed outlook, she found the motivation to persist with her new way of directing herself in activity, which was founded on the use of her reasoning processes. And as she did this, so her ability to act on her recognition of cognitive distortions increased. She began to feel comfortable selling her work, increasingly confident that people were spending their cash because they liked what they saw. In this, Vicky actually began to bridge the gap between idea and deed.

Many students have experiences like Vicky, in that when they make a constructive change, buried feelings come to the surface, sometimes associated with long-forgotten memories. On the plus side, when this happens in a lesson, we tend to find that a person is better able to accommodate their uncomfortable feelings, even if they grow stronger, when they stop creating physical distortions in themselves. However, in the last analysis, it will always be up to the student to decide. For, if there is a place they long to go, a dream they desire to fulfill, and, as they make the changes necessary to reach it, they are beset with uncomfortable, unwanted feelings, they can choose to go back, or carry on. They can, metaphorically, reach for the bottle once more, or jump on the wagon and ride.

In this connection, Walter Carrington, F M Alexander's teaching assistant in London for many, many years, says that the best way to find something lost is to tidy up.[5] And, having followed this advice for the last several years, I can wholeheartedly recommend it. Likewise, when we start tidying things up in lessons, although we do not know what we will find, we may discover something that as far as we were concerned was lost. In much the same way, if you go up into a messy attic and start tidying up, all sorts of long-forgotten things may appear. Or nothing at all. In some cases, the thing you wanted or were scared to find has by now disintegrated. All that remains is a cob-web and dust.

The important point here is that you cannot know in advance what you will find. To keep going forward, you must be prepared to take a step into the unknown. And to do that, you must trust in the path you are taking.[6]

In practice, we find that students only acquire the conviction necessary to carry on, in spite of feeling wrong, when they finally trust in their reasoning processes. For it is their reasoning processes that have led them to this point, and they see well enough that to make further progress they must continue working to the principles they have reasoned out. They must continue with this new, conscious (reasoning) direction of themselves irrespective of what they feel.

In virtually all of the aforementioned examples, whether it was Sid sitting, or Philip walking, whether it was a singer singing, or a trumpeter trumpeting, whether it was Alexander reciting, or me attempting to read my own work on stage, we were considering a specific task or activity. However, each of these examples illustrates a truth that can be applied to our lives as a whole, and that is that significant inner change is at some point almost always accompanied by uncomfortable feelings. Quite simply, most of us find it troubling, or disconcerting, to *feel wrong*, in the sense of unfamiliar, as we go about our business. Even the sudden experience of joy, or pleasure, or freedom, or relief from continual discomfort, if it shows no sign of abating, can awaken in us a feeling of worry, or dread. And in my case at least, I have recognised that this type of feeling is one I don't like to feel. When presented with a new experience of myself (as a consequence of changing the way I direct myself in activity), it has often been a case of, "better the devil you know," than taking a bold step into the unknown.

In speaking of this, I would like to say a few words about a popular self-help book written by Dr Susan Jeffers, entitled: "Feel the Fear and Do It Anyway," which I was recommended to read by Don Weed.

In this helpful little book, as I recall, Dr Jeffers focuses her attention on helping people to get on and just "do it anyway" in spite of their fears; she outlines strategies for not letting fear prevent us from undertaking challenges, whether public-speaking, intimacy, taking responsibility for ourselves, or pushing ourselves to new and better things in our lives. All well and good. On the down side, the issue of how a student will sometimes change themselves in response to their fear is left largely untouched. However, in teaching Alexander's work, how a person changes their manner of response when they feel scared, rather than their failure to make a response, is, for the majority of students, the greatest obstacle to progress. And this is because so many people create additional distortions in themselves in their attempts to diminish or accommodate their fears.

You may remember Willie Thorne, who often underperformed on the verge of momentous success. Willie's (presumed) anxiety did not stop him from performing; his (presumed) fear did not give him reason to give up. Instead, Willie responded to the prospect of winning by changing something in himself, which had the effect of disabling him as one of the world's greatest players. For Willie, and everyone like him, to make headway, he must either change his ideas about tournament success, so that the prospect of winning does not give him reason to respond so badly, or he has to learn to continue at his usual standard, irrespective of what he feels. In both scenarios, he has to work on his ideas.

"The fear will never go away so long as I continue to grow."

Susan Jeffers

In practice, if you are someone, like me, who experiences fear when you think your inner world is about to change dramatically, then you will find that, in the long run at least, it is more productive to learn to change your response to fear, rather than to eradicate ideas that are associated with a particular fear. For, as Dr Jeffers succinctly writes: "The fear will never go away so long as I continue to grow."[7]

If, as I do, you wish to chart a course of on-going improvement, then at some point, if you haven't done so already, you will need to make friends with fear. For the fear will never go away, not if you continue to grow, not if you continue to improve.

In this connection, I remember an interview with Billy Connolly, the world-famous comedian, who was asked to describe how he feels moments before walking out in front of a new audience for the first time. In reply, he said that if he didn't feel nervous, if he didn't feel wobbly inside with butterflies in his tummy, then he knew something was wrong. For feeling scared in the face of the unknown is a normal and appropriate response. In fact, I have always been told by the very best performers, whether athletes, sports-people, actors, singers or comedians, that the feeling of anxiety before or during performance did not go away as they became more successful and respected. For these people, feeling fear simply became reason to perform well rather than reason to sabotage themselves. We can all learn from their experience. For there is nothing wrong in feeling scared: fear is a legitimate response. If, however, we allow our discomfort in feeling scared to dominate our performance, we will either give up and go home, or introduce such distortions in ourselves that we can no longer perform at our best.

On the subject of comedians, the other day I heard an interview on the radio with Pamela Stephenson – Billy's wife and biographer - who, as my British readers will no doubt recall, used to star in the highly successful and influential TV comedy, *Not The Nine O'Clock News*. These days, Ms Stephenson cheerfully reported, she works as a psychotherapist in California, and in the course of the interview she described how it felt to make such a big change in the direction of her life.

If I remember rightly, she talked of an initial experience of being in free-fall, when all the usual structures in her life disappeared. She had given up so many of the things that gave her life its characteristic shape and feel, she had the impression of quite literally falling freely through the air; an experience, no doubt, either terrifying or exhilarating, according to your taste.

In much the same way, if you have followed my argument to this point, if you are minded to work to the principles I have outlined in this book, then you must be prepared, at some point, for a similar experience. Be prepared, at the very least, to step into the unknown.

In this connection, Frank Pierce Jones says that: "the hallmark of the Alexander Technique is a kinesthetic feeling of lightness." In my view, he is both right and wrong in this. Right, insofar as so many people experience a feeling of lightness in activity when they stop creating distortions in themselves; right, in that so many people experience a loss of the usual heaviness that gives their world its characteristic feel; but wrong insofar as what any one particular person will experience when they walk down the path Alexander mapped out is ultimately unknown and unknowable.

Milan Kundera, the Czech novelist, entitles one of his books, *The Unbearable Lightness of Being.* For me, that sums up very well an experience I sometimes have when I stop creating obstacles in my own path. Then, life really does seem so easy, to have lost all of it's usual shape and fixture, to involve too little effort; at such moments, life itself really can strike me as being unbearably light, at least for a while. But importantly, what you yourself will feel if you work to the principles outlined in this book is anyone's guess. The only thing we can be reasonably sure of is that your experience of yourself will change. In this, you will encounter the new. And to sustain your confidence in this encounter, what you most need is trust, a genuine trust that does not require the presence or absence of certain feelings.[9]

Notes

1. To be found in Notes of Instruction in *The Alexander Technique - The Essencial Writings of F M Alexander*, selected by Ed Maisel.

2. pg. 85, *The Use of the Self*.

3. *Man's Supreme Inheritance*.

4. pg. 45, *The Use of the Self*.

5. *Explaining the Alexander Technique*, Walter Carington in conversation with Sean Carey.

6. This is not to say you should blindly accept everything the teacher, or someone in the group watching says they see or hear as the gospel truth. On the contrary, you need to learn to trust in your reasoning processes, in your ability to make judgements on the basis of an open-minded assessment of the facts, over and above whatever it is you feel.

7. pg. 22, *Feel the Fear and Do It Anyway*.

8. *The Artist's Way*.

9. However, when I say that trust is necessary in Alexander's work, when I tell you that you need to cultivate a genuine trust that does not require the assurance of feeling right if you are to reach the desination we have all long been headed, when, what is more, I quote Julia Cameron who says: "Jump and the net will appear!" please remember that I am not asking you for blind faith, no, not at all. Instead, I am asking you jump across a ravine your reasoning processes have indicated you can comfortably bridge. I am asking you to trust in your reasoning mind. For, just like Leif riding his bicycle without stabilizers, like Philip taking that first new step, like Vicky selling a painting and believing the buyer really wanted it, like Alexander reciting on stage without his habitual misdirection, like me, for that matter, learning to write fiction again as an adult, we have all had to trust, but not trust blindly. No, we have had to trust in something we believed was true, in something that, on some level, in whatever way, appealed to our conscious minds. In something that made sense to us. And it was this trust, however shaky it was intitially, that gave us the conviction necessary to carry on, even on those occasions when we heard a voice crying out, "No, this is wrong!"

Ten

Working to Principle

walking the path you have chosen

"Be patient; stick to principle; and it will all open up like a great cauliflower."
- A R Alexander[1]

In this, the final chapter of my book, I shall outline a way for building on the achievements you have made, so that you can continue this journey for yourself, and thereby bring about ongoing and lasting improvements in everything you do. I will do this by exploring what it means to work to principle in the performance of each and every task, as opposed to mechanically following a fixed set of rules.

But first, I should like to address a few words to the student who arrives at this point honestly believing that I have so far failed to give them a decent answer to the question that continues to tax them, for they are still unclear about what it is they should do. Perhaps, not surprisingly, I tend to see things differently. From my vantage-point, rather than my failure to address this particular concern, it seems to me that this particular student did not like the answers I gave, that I will continue to give, as our destination swings into view. For, if a student has improved, if they are continuing to make constructive changes in themselves, then it is my sincere conviction that they can help themselves most by continuing to explore the application of these principles in their lives.

"But I don't *know* how," a student will sometimes protest,

more often than not when they have just succeeded in making a huge improvement in an activity that matters to them a great deal.

"Have you made improvements so far?"

"Yes, but I worry I don't know how to keep going."

"Well, if you have made improvements so far, then maybe you do in fact know how, only this kind of *knowing* does not match the *knowing* you want."

"Yes, yes, I understand that. My problem is that I don't see how to go on making constructive changes in myself. How do I do that? How does anyone do that? How do you?"

"I work to principle. I seek to live my life according to principles I have reasoned out."

"You do?"

"Yes. The improvements I have enjoyed to date have arisen by my going to work with an improved and improving set of rules. In order to continue to get better, I seek to work to principle in whatever it is I do."

"But you haven't really answered my question, because I still don't know what to do."

"In that case, we need to go back to the beginning once more and go over some of the ground we have covered."

In the very first section, you may recall, we talked about the different meanings of the word *principle*. There, I said that I was primarily interested in principles as rules that could be applied to any or every action. Now, however, as we press on towards the end of our journey, we need to make the distinction between principle on the one hand and procedure (or practice) on the other. As far as this distinction goes, a principle is a rule (in the sense of guide-line), and a procedure is something you do to comply with the rule.

In teaching Alexander's work, for example, if the principle is *begin with the end in mind*, then a procedure consistent with this principle would be to start the lesson by asking the student what it is they hope to achieve. The principle suggests a way of going to work; the procedure is what you do.

As another example, in English Law we have the following principle, *the burden of proof lies with the prosecution*, and a practice consistent with this principle is that a defendant is not obliged to say anything in their own defence. The principle suggests what you do; the procedure is what you do.

Unfortunately, the matter is sometimes confused because, on occasion, we use the word *rule* to mean convention, or fixed procedure. For example, in chess, we say that one of the rules is that the player with the white pieces moves first. However, this is not a rule in the sense of principle or guide-line, but a convention. Likewise, one of the rules at Leif's school is not to run down the corridors. Clearly, this is not a principle; it's simply a rule that has consequences if and when ignored. So, although principles can be thought of as rules, it would be a mistake to think of all rules as principles.

When working to principle, there is always some reasoning to do.

When I talk about principles, therefore, I am more often than not talking about rules that can be applied. In this sense, working to principle can be contrasted with the implementation of a fixed and unyielding procedure. When working to principle, there is always some reasoning to do.

Consider the following example.

Recently, a friend of mine got work at a call-centre. It was his job to give out information to callers. One day, someone happened to phone up asking where they could buy an extremely rare toy in Bristol. By coincidence, my friend had spent the weekend trying to buy just such a toy for his son. After a long and arduous search, he had discovered the only toy-shop in Bristol that stocked them. Consequently, he typed the name of the toy-shop into his computer, pressed *search*, and gave the caller the number that flashed up on his screen. He then went on to the next call.

A little while later, he was summoned into the supervisor's office.

"It has come to my attention that you have not been following the procedure for dealing with retail enquiries."

"Excuse me?"

"If someone wants to buy a toy in Bristol, what is the first thing you must do?"

"But this case was different."

"*Step one* is we search toy-shops in Bristol."

"But…"

"Listen, I did not call you in for a debate. The next infringement will result in a written warning."

"That's not fair."

"It's not a question of fair. I'm just doing what it says in the book. These are the rules."

My friend was reprimanded for not following the standard procedure. But on this occasion, following the procedure just didn't make sense. We can be reasonably certain, however, that there was in fact a principle underlying the creation of this procedure; in all likelihood it was *time is money*. We can easily see how a procedure of this kind would ordinarily help to save time. But not on this occasion; in this instance, the rigid application of the procedure would actually have meant a loss of time. My friend could see that following the procedure mechanically would have sabotaged the underlying principle.

In all areas of life, we see this phenomenon repeatedly. Often it gives us occasion to laugh; sometimes, however, the consequences are more serious. Consider the following.

Many years ago, my Mum was ill in hospital, so my Dad had to do the supermarket shopping. Finding no empty spaces in the car-park, he decided to park his car on a yellow line outside the store, confident he could get the job done in under five minutes. However, ten minutes had passed and he had barely got half way through his list. Worse, there were long queues at the check-outs. He began to worry about his car, so he hurried out of the shop (with the shopping-basket) to see if could now find a space in the car-park.

The next thing he knew he was being manhandled by a security guard and taken back into the store. The guard and the store-manager were accusing him of stealing.

Ten minutes later, two police-men arrived. They asked my Dad to explain himself, so he told them exactly what had happened and how the whole thing was a big mistake.

On thinking the matter over, one of the police-men asked to see the shopping-list. Sure enough, only half the items on the list were in the basket. Next, the other police-man asked my Dad what money he had on him. My Dad opened his wallet displaying cards and cash. Satisfied, the police-men told the store-manager that the police would not be pressing charges, as there was no evidence that a deliberate theft had taken place. They told the security-guard my Dad was free to go. At this point, my Dad, the police-men and the security-guard all thought the case was closed. But the store-manager had other ideas.

"If you're not going to press charges, then we will," he said.

"Why?" asked one of the police-men. "There's no hope of securing a conviction. It looks every bit like an honest mistake."

"At this store, we have a policy that all suspected shop-lifters will be prosecuted, regardless of the circumstances. This man is a suspected shop-lifter and therefore he must be prosecuted. It doesn't make any difference to me if it was a legitimate mistake or not. We have a clear procedure in such cases, and it is my duty to ensure it is followed to the letter."

"Very well," said the police-man, "but don't expect any help from us."

Again, what we have here is the fixed or rigid application of a procedure, so that the original principle is lost. Instead of the supermarket succeeding in creating the impression that they are tough on shop-lifters, they have created the impression (at least to me) that they are inflexible, vindictive and stupid.*

In spite of the above, however, I am not arguing against procedures or systems. On the contrary. As someone who has man-

"In teaching, the first essential should be to cultivate the uses of the mind and body and not, as is so often the case, to neglect the instrument of thought and reason by the inculcation of fixed rules."

F M Alexander

---

* About three months later, my Dad was finally in court. After listening to the evidence of the security-guard, and hearing the testimony of my Dad, the magistrate found in my Dad's favour. This time, the case was finally laid to rest.

aged staff, I know only too well their value. I can confidently assert that it is impossible to run a business, or teach a class, without following procedures. The problem is not with procedures *per se*, but with following procedures rigidly, for there will always be times when the rigid adoption of a procedure fails us, for the simple reason that our world is constantly changing. For this reason, on-going improvement in life requires that we understand the principles underpinning the procedures we are following. Indeed, when we have reached such a stage in our development, we will be able to invent new procedures according to the demands of the situations we face. To that end, in each chapter of the book, I have given examples of both working to and not working to the various principles in question, and I could easily give more.

In chapter one, for example, we learned that Alexander began his investigation believing his problem was physical, and for that reason he sought a physical solution to his physical ills. Later, he adopted the principle of psycho-physical unity, and from then on he directed his efforts towards changing what he sometimes referred to as his *thinking in activity* in order to generate the improvements he sought. Likewise, for the student who wants to improve the dynamic relationship of their head to their body in activity, we can say that they will be employing this principle (as I have presented it) when they go to work on the thinking that generates their movement behaviour, and not when they seek out someone to correctly align their head.

In chapter two, for example, I introduced the principle of the use of reason. Alexander cited the example of Carlyle, who, in an attempt to save Henry Taylor, had rushed from London to Sheen with a bottle of medicine that had done Mrs Carlyle good, without knowing for what the medicine was useful. This was an example of not working to the principle (of the use of reason). As an example of working to the principle, I told you about the student who, when faced with the problem of the monkey-trap, decides to let go of the nut and then turns the bottle up-side down to tip it out.

In chapter 3, for example, we decided that, as a first step, when there was something about our performance we wanted to improve, we would seek to eliminate self-generated interference, as opposed to adding corrective movements in. We called this working to the principle of prevention.

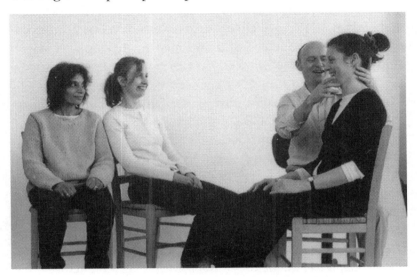

In chapter 4, we concluded that the habit of flying from one extreme to another was associated with mistaking effects for causes. To that end, we would be working to this principle when we went to work on the cause(s) of our unwanted response, and not when we when we directed our energies to modifying the unwanted effects. So that, if we notice we are pulling our head back and down, we do not attempt to push it forward and up.

In chapter 5, for example, we recognised that we would be working to the principle of feelings are unreliable when we judged our relative success or failure according to the standard of our performance, and not on the basis of what or how we felt. To that end, if we have the impression that we have stopped interfering with the poise of the head in relation to the body in activity, we will seek some objective evidence before concluding that we really have stopped.

In chapter 6, for example, we high-lighted the principle of

fixed, preconceived ideas. We concluded that a person who sought to continue this journey according to their current point of view, without a willingness or readiness to change it, would not be working to this principle. On the contrary, on-going and lasting improvement requires that we are willing to change our paradigms in the light of new experience. To that end, when we are working to this principle, we freely examine our preconceptions and our prejudices, and are open to making a paradigm shift. In practice, we can work to this principle by acknowledging that "thinking may not be what we think it is," and not by insisting that our current idea of right is terminally right, irrespective of any new evidence we may find.

In chapter 7, we introduced the principle of the most effective way. We said that we would be employing this principle if we identified the steps we needed to take to reach our destination, and not when we set off without a plan, relying instead on on a roll of the dice. We would be working to this principle if we employed a protocol appropriate to the task at hand, and not if we approached a given task in a random or haphazard way.

In chapter 8, we identified the principle of mental discipline. We said that we would be employing this principle when we worked to break down our fixed habits of thought, and not when we sought to build an ever-increasing reliance on the proficiency of our automatic recall. In practice, we could work to this principle by adopting the procedure Alexander named *inhibition*, as opposed to always continuing to do whatever feels natural.

In chapter 9, we introduced the principle of genuine trust. We said that we would be working to this principle when we gave up trying to feel right, and instead persisted with principles we had reasoned out. In practice, we could employ this principle by sticking with a reasoned protocol for performing a task, even if a voice from somewhere deep inside us screamed, "No, this is wrong!"

In each chapter, I gave examples of when we would be working to the principle and when not. My intention was to convey the principle in such a way that, when faced with a new and different situation, the potential application would be clear. As a consequence, I have avoided giving specific instructions that could be applied to the performance of any or every task.

I do recognise, however, that for some students the task of linking up the various principles in this book to the fulfillment of their aspiration is easier said than done, as this final principle, the principle of *working to principle*, is new.

In this connection, one of my students, Alicia, recently said to me: "Didn't Alexander figure out a set of procedures based upon his principles? If so, what are they? Can't you just tell me the practical procedures so that I can do them? Why can't you just tell me what to do?"

Sadly, we live in an age when most of us have become habituated to being spoon-fed winning formulas for success, to being handed down set procedures for dealing with the problems we face. As a consequence, the idea of working to principle to make constructive changes in ourselves represents a fundamental shift in our point of view. For example, if we suffer from general poor health, then we are advised to change our diet or go to the gym. If we are feeling stressed, then we are advised we should practise relaxation techniques, or in more serious cases, a course of psychotherapy, or even tranquillizing drugs. As a consequence, a great many people are looking for a recipe, in the sense of a set of instructions, for improvement. When it comes to making changes in themselves, they have come to expect a list of do's and don'ts. The idea of working to principle - which involves giving up depending on fixed procedures – is completely foreign. For this reason, the principle of *working to principle* presents students like Alicia with a problem. They would prefer it if they could just be told what to do. However, that is not the course I am teaching. In fact, I can't give you a set of instructions and be true to my own beliefs; it is my conviction that I can serve you best by helping you to decide for yourself the best course for you.

"If you apply the principle to the carrying out of one evolution, you have learned the lot."

F M Alexander

In saying this, I am not claiming that we cannot enjoy improvements by following procedures without understanding the principle that underpins them. Far from it. There are a great many things that can be taught to students to bring about instant and in some cases lasting improvements. For example, if the student has a problem carrying a ruck-sack, caused in large part because they are wearing it half-way down their back, then the teacher can advise them to pull the straps forward, so that the distance of the bag from the shoulders is reduced. Immediately, the student will find that the bag is easier to carry. However, if the student does not understand why, if they have not grasped the underlying principle, then we will almost certainly find them running into the same problem when they pick up their duffel-bag. It is not that the teaching of set procedures is in itself a defective approach; simply that when students learn procedures without understanding the principles behind them, they cannot go on to map out a path of on-going improvement for themselves. It is the difference between giving someone a fish to eat, and teaching them how to fish.*

As you might expect, Alexander did in fact work out a number of practical procedures that followed from his principles, and he made use of them in the classes that he taught. However, he also recognised that if you blindly follow any procedure without understanding the principle that underpins it, the procedure will in time become fixed, and thereby prevent you from making on-going improvements in whatever it is you do. Of much more importance, in this regard, is that the student understand the principle of working to principle, for then the student will be able to adapt themselves to each and every task. Indeed, in his

---

* However, for a student who is dying of hunger, we might well want to begin by giving them a fish. You see, in my class, even the practice of teaching principles will not be taught rigidly, for we can always imagine a scenario when any given principle - no matter how basic or universal it appears to be - will fail to apply.

last book, F M wrote:

"A person who learns to work to a principle in doing one exercize will have learned to do all exercizes, but the person who learns to "do an exercize" will most assuredly have to go on learning exercizes *ad infinitum*."[2]

To that end, if a student reaches the end of the course and says, "I truly don't know how to carry on," what they are most likely saying is that the application of the principles is not sufficiently clear to them. They cannot figure out – at least to a standard that meets their approval - the practical application.

At this point, I will usually remind my students that, in a first course, all we set out to gain was a basic understanding of Alexander's technique. To that extent, acquiring a basic familiarity with his principles, and the beginnings of a competence in their application represents a huge achievement. For these are new and immensely challenging ideas. We do not seek complete mastery on our first acquaintance, even if mastery is our ultimate goal. For Alexander's work is concerned with the process of on-going improvement. We are more interested in the idea of journey than in arriving in any one place.

"Don't you see that if you 'get' perfection today, you will be farther away from perfection than you have ever been."

F M Alexander

Throughout this journey, our primary concern has been improvement. To that end, if you want to continue to make changes in your life, then fixed procedures alone will not help you. In time, they will send you backwards. For that reason, I have included no exercizes, or self-help procedures. On the contrary, I am urging you to seek to understand the principles I am teaching, rather than adopting a fixed set of rules that I or anyone else have judged to be useful.

If you come to my class, however, there might very well be a great many things I would advise you to do. For example, keeping a journal, reading books, experimenting with the ideas in relation to everyday tasks, endeavouring to explain what you are learning to others. All these things can help you.

However, to really set ourselves free, we must figure out the application of these principles for ourselves. This means that if we believe our problem is an on-going deterioration in our general standard of performance, we must adopt procedures for raising our general standard that make sense to us, that appeal to our reasoning minds. We will not commit to a set of excerizes just because someone tells us they will do us good. Likewise, if you try to employ these principles willy-nilly, without troubling yourself to understand the thinking that underpins them, you will not be working to principle of working to principle. This is a vitally important point. We must endeavour to understand each principle and not mechanically follow the procedure that follows from it if we are to bring about on-going and lasting improvements in our lives.

"Okay, I see the need to work to principle, I'm finally persuaded of that. But I still have questions, for instance:

Do I need to employ specific principles for specific situations, or do I need to use all the principles all the time?

And:

Is is possible for the principles to contradict each other? I mean, could one principle suggest one course of action and a different principle another. If so, what do you do then?"

These are wonderful questions. If a student should get to the end of the course and be asking questions like these, then, from my vantage-point, the course has almost certainly been a success. In an attempt to answer them, let me begin by saying this.

A great deal of the world's practical wisdom is expressed in the form of idiomatic sayings or adages. For example, we have all heard: "a bird in the hand is worth two in the bush," "two heads are better than one," "strike while the iron is hot." These adages are expressions of principles as timeless as ourselves.

In this connection, I recently heard a radio journalist say that for every piece of advice conveyed by an adage, there is another adage advising the opposing course. For example, we are sometimes told, "if you look after the pennies, the pounds will look after themselves," but we also hear, "penny-wise, pound foolish." How do we reconcile these sayings? Surely they are recommending different things? Likewise, we are told, "two heads are better than one," but also, "too many cooks spoil the broth." Surely one saying is recommending one course, and the other saying other? To that extent, aren't all these sayings useless? For you can always find an adage recommending any course you want to take.

My view, perhaps unsurprisingly, is no, not at all; and that's because every single principle, even the use of reason or psycho-physical unity, has a limited application. The problem identified by the radio journalist only arises when people seek to apply principles mechanically, and ignore the circumstance they are in.

By way of an example, in business, we can easily imagine someone telling themselves "penny-wise, pound foolish," and so ignoring the fact they are losing a small amount of money on a very large number of transactions, and hence, over time, going bankrupt. As every bank-manager will tell you, the pennies always mount up. When something happens again and again and again, the very small will almost always become the very big. In business, as in teaching, this is an important principle. Likewise, we can imagine a business person becoming so fixated on the minor financial details of a deal, that they fail to recognise that they are being fleeced somewhere else in the transaction for a much more significant amount. In fact, it is a failure to grasp this principle that leads so many people to make un-sound purchases, for they attend only to the price-tag, and so forget to read the small print at the bottom of the page. In the ITM, we sometimes refer to this phenomenon as a failure to keep the big picture in mind.

In every endeavour in life, both the principle of *small things add up*, and *keeping the big picture in mind* are important. However, according to the circumstance we are in, their relative importance will vary. For example, in chess, it is said that the former world champion Gary Kasparov won his games by accumulating tiny positional advantages steadily move by move. Eventually, his positional advantage becomes so big, he could easily convert it into a tactical win. To have any chance of success, his opponents had to counter this strategy, often by employing it themselves.

Over the years, I have often seen weaker players employ this very strategy quite brilliantly, so that they build up a huge positional advantage, only to forget that their opponent is about to take their king. And since winning in chess is all about the taking the opponents king, all their hard work comes to nought.

We see a similar phenomenon in snooker. Most players will tell you that the key to success in control of the cue-ball. The best players in the world seem to move it around the table as if it were attached to their cue on a piece of string. However, even the top players will, on occasion, become so fixated on getting the white ball exactly where they want it for the next shot in their break, that they forget to make the pot, and as a consequence lose the game.

"I have never found two cases exactly alike, and the detailed instructions which I might lay down for A might be extremely detrimental to B and C."

F M Alexander

Sadly, a great many people live their lives failing to grasp this principle. In their attempts to attend to what is important, they overlook what is yet more important still. To that extent, the problem is not that our idiomatic sayings, or the various principles in Alexander's work, might on occasion appear to suggest different courses of action; rather, the problem is in recognising the appropriateness of their application according to the situations we face. For example, I once heard a debate about Alexander's principle of prevention in the context of dieting. The claim was made the Alexandrian way of losing weight was to stop eating the wrong things, rather than trying to add the right things in. Clearly, such advice could be dangerous in the extreme, according to the condition of the dieter. It results from seeking to extend the application of an idea to a situation for which it was never intended.

The relative importance of Alexander's principles will vary from situation to situation. For example, one student may be most stymied by lacking an appropriate protocol for the task before them, whereas another may be most hampered by their desire to feel right in the gaining of their end. Indeed, the relative importance of Alexander's principles may at times vary for the same student according to the task with which they are engaged.

All the principles are important, however. They all have a role to play in helping us to move from where we are now to somewhere better.[3]

Recognising the appropriateness of a principle to the situations we face requires not only that we understand the thinking behind the principle, but it also requires judgement. And our judgement improves as we gain and reflect upon our experiences. To that extent, building sound judgement takes time. We cannot acquire a complete and total mastery on the very first day. At the end of a ten-week course, familiarity and the beginnings of a competence in the application of these basic principles is, for most students, a more realistic and achievable goal.

I have no desire to dent the enthusiasm of the ambitious, but for most us, the change involved in giving up the habits of a life-time takes time to fully embrace. In practice, the benefits we can accrue are enormous, when we begin to apply these principles in our lives.

In the very first section, if you remember, we talked about building a bridge in stages, and I gave the example of Brunel flying his kite over the Avon Gorge. So it is with Alexander's technique: there are stages we need to pass through to effectively learn and apply the principles upon which his work is based. We cannot reasonably expect anyone to master the application of these principles overnight. An important first step is simply recognising the various principles and their potential applications. In this regard, you will likely find that some of the principles in this book strike you as obvious and easy; others as incomprehensible or irrelevant, according to your past experience. Indeed, your understanding of the principles themselves will very likely change as you continue the voyage by yourself.

In the course of this journey, I have outlined ten basic principles derived from the teachings of F M Alexander. If you can succeed in learning how to direct yourself in activity in a manner consistent with these principles, you will have discovered a means for putting Alexander's important discovery to work in your life. If you do this, you can bring about lasting and ongoing improvements in everything you do.

But we cannot do this by relying on a fixed set of procedures, just as we must give up attempting to direct ourselves in activity according to fixed habits of thought. No, we must instead acquire the discipline of working to principle in the daily course of our lives. If we do this, we will encounter that freedom and flexibility in ourselves necessary to thrive in changing times. If we do this, we will begin to discover the wherewithal for translating our best ideas into deeds.

And all we need to do now is to continue putting one foot after the next. We must walk the path we have chosen.

Notes

1. pg. 68, *Freedom to Change.*
2. pg. 164, *The Universal Constant in Living.*
3. In almost every field of human endeavour, whether it is acting or martial arts, whether it is carpentry or running a business, whether it is cooking or self-help, there are basic principles and accompanying procedures that need to be learned and applied. In every single discipline, over time a body of knowledge that constitutes good practice is gradually established. We sometimes refer to procedures equated with good practice as *the tricks of the trade.* For example, in the movie business, junior script-writers are told not to kill off their best characters in the opening scenes, and, in Hollywood at least, that their script has a much greater chance of being made into a movie if it has a happy ending.

In this connection, I once saw an interview with the film director, Quentin Tarantino, during which he re-lived a telephone call with his producer regarding his proposed script for *Pulp Fiction.* As I recall it, the conversation Tarantino relayed went something like this.

"Quentin, I'm reading your script here and we got a problem, a big problem."

"Oh, what's that?"

"Well, I'm only half-way through, and you've just killed off the guy everyone's going to love, you know, the guy you want Travolta to play. Quentin, you know I have a major problem with you doing something like that."

"Don't worry. It's not what it seems."

"You mean he comes back to life? After all those bullets?"

"No, it's a time thing. That scene is not where you think it is. The character comes back to play a scene that took place earlier. You see, I show the events out of sequence."

"I'm not sure I follow, Quentin, so just tell me this: do we see the Travolta character in the last scene of the film?"

"Yes."

"Does he have a smile on his face?"

"Yes."

"Then I'm happy, Quentin. Problem solved."

Luckily for Tarantino, his producer is able to see past the rigid adoption of a fixed procedure, one that as a rule forbids the film-maker to kill off his best characters till the end. The producer recognises that Tarantino can stick with the principle of preserving the best character and jettison the standard procedure. This is because he understands the thinking behind the principle. To that extent he can employ it creatively. The principle opens up possibilities rather than closing them down. We see the same thing in applying Alexander's principles to the various tasks of life. Those students who really understand the principles are not stuck with a set of fixed procedures; on the contrary, students who have truly understood the principles will be able to decide for themselves specific applications in their lives. And all I am saying is that an ability to do this consistently and well takes judgement. And building judgment takes time. It is not necessary (or possible) to understand the whole of Alexander's work at the end of an initial ten-week course. We will build our judgement slowly step by step.

In making a successful movie, just as in any pursuit in life, there are a great many principles to consider. For example, in the horror film, *Jaws*, Stephen Spielberg chose to have the shark kill a small boy first as a way of unsettling his audience early, an important principle in films of this genre. His thinking was: if they're prepared to kill an innocent child, there's no limit to what they might do. In this way, he lets his audience know they aren't to relax. In the event, killing an innocent child was a break with the Hollywood horror-film convention of the time, and became a powerful tool in Spielberg's hands for unsettling the audience in the early stages of the film.

Likewise, in the film, *Deep Blue Sea*, the character played by Samuel L Jackson - who is *Pulp Fiction*'s other favourite character – is killed by a shark in the opening stages. Immediately, the film has placed itself outside Hollywood's standard conventions. No one, certainly not me, was expecting that. From there on, I am prepared to believe that anything might happen. Unfortunately, however, in following that procedure, which is a simple variation of the one used by Spielberg in *Jaws*, the film violated another Hollywood principle, namely, that you preserve your best characters till the end. And in my judgement, this second principle carried more weight on the day. For, as soon as it became apparent that Mr Jackson was not coming back, I lost interest in the film and gave up watching. In all likelihood, I was not alone in being someone who had no interest once my favourite character was dead. To that extent, in making a horror-film, both of these principles, namely, *preserving favourite characters* and *unsettling the audience early* are important; however, deciding which carries most weight will depend upon a judgement made case by case on the day.

In film-making, as in any endeavour, the difference between competence and mastery lies in the ability to make a sound judgement about the relative importance of a principle to the task. This is what separates the novice from the master. In this regard, Stephen Spielberg's judgement is phenomenal. When making a Hollywood movie, he knows exactly which principles and accompanying procedures to employ to obtain his desired effect.

In speaking of this, I am reminded of an interview I once read with former World Chess Champion, Anatoly Karpov. The interviewer began: "There are many hundreds of grandmasters in the world today, but only one world champion. What makes the difference between the top players and a player like you."

Mr Karpov responded something like this: "All grandmasters understand the principles of chess, for example, striving to take control of the central squares in the opening, developing the rooks on open files, keeping a balance of control over both the white and the black squares, making your pieces work as a team instead of having them conduct operations alone, exchanging pieces so that your pawns are left in lines and not left stranded by themselves. And so on and so on. I could give you a very long list. All grandmasters have learned these principles and have mastered how to apply them creatively in their games. What separates these players from a player like me is this: I can see so deeply into a position that I recognise when it would be better to ignore an established principle because an even more fundamental principle applies. This, I believe, is what gives me a competitive edge. I will sometimes play moves the others would never dream of playing; I will play moves that will surprise them; I will play moves that to them don't look right."

In playing chess, Mr Karpov understands the rules so well he can break them. At his best, his judgement was second to none. In this, his mastery was all but complete.

Closing Words

"The difficulty for all of us is to take up a new way of life in which we must apply principles instead of the haphazard end-gaining methods of the past. This indicates a slow process and we must all be content with steady improvements from day to day."
- F M Alexander[1]

We began with a goal and the recognition that we needed to be willing to undergo change in order to reach it. We have now arrived at the end of this particular journey.

Along the way, we decided that we needed to engage our minds with the task of changing our thinking to stop sending ourselves wrong in the carrying out of a plan we have reasoned out. To do this, we have begun to build the mental discipline necessary to walk through the critical moment and beyond. We have begun to cultivate a genuine trust in the path we are taking, so much so that we are not tempted to give up whenever we feel wrong. All that is required now is that we carry on walking. Yes, we just need to continue sailing the seven seas.

In practice, we can work to the principle of the unity of thought and action, or separation; to the principle of thinking things through, or acting in a random and haphazard way; to the principle of prevention, or cure. We can choose to do the opposite of what we believe we are doing wrong; we can try to rely upon our feelings for guidance; we can go to work on the basis of our fixed, preconceived ideas. Or not. We get to choose.

We can reason out an effective means for fulfilling our aspirations; we can work to build the mental discipline to walk through the critical moment and beyond; we can cultivate a genuine trust in the principles we have reasoned out. We can endeavour to work to principle in everything we do. Or not. We get to choose.

The principles in this book are designed to help you to move forward. It is up to you to put them to work. No one can do it for you. You must do the work yourself. You must find your own solution to the monkey-trap. And you can. If you want to get better, you must change the rules you live by. You must work to a new set of principles if you would bring about improvements in everything you do. And the principles in this book really can help you. They arise from an open-minded study of thinking in relation to movement. They can help you to apply Alexander's important discovery in your life.

I said in the opening chapter that the sequence of the principles in this book was not fixed. I could have begun and finished elsewhere; I have could have suggested a different pathway. However, as I have engaged with the issue of improvement in my own life, and in teaching improvement to others, I have discovered this particular way of climbing the ladder; it is a way of bridging the gap between idea and deed. It is a pathway that has and continues to work for me. It is inspired by the teachings of F M Alexander, in the main taught to me by Dr Donald L Weed. To that end, what I have presented you with in this book is simply a way in. Once you have mastered it, you can put it to one side, and then begin the task of identifying your own principles and sequencing them for yourself. For, if you work to the principles I have described in this book, without eventually making them your own, then the benefits you will gain will be limited. You may well end up living my dream instead of yours. And ultimately, it is the fulfillment of your aspiration that matters.

To gain a complete control of your own potentialities, you must figure out something for yourself. There is no other way. And you can. Believe me, you can. Even if, from where you are starting now, the road ahead looks daunting. Even if, you have little idea where to begin. For in the pages of F M's books, or in those written by Don Weed, and in this one, there are pointers to get you started, foot-holds for you to begin scaling the rocks.

"Do not trouble your-self about going slow-ly; it is necessary to go slowly."

A R Alexander[3]

The process of understanding these principles is cumulative, in that our understanding of them gradually increases, as does our ability to apply them. In Alexander's work, we do not need to know or understand everything before we can begin. No, our understanding grows as we experiment and engage with the ideas. We can continue to get better by simply putting one foot after the next.

Isamard Kingdom Brunel began building the Clifton Suspension Bridge by flying a kite attached to a ball of string. I got to the centre of the maze by going back to the beginning and starting again. The monkey got his nut by letting go of the one in the bottle and wandering off to find one lying on the ground. To get better, all you need is a change of heart, a change of course. The solution to the problem of your life lies within. If, however, you are stuck for a way of moving forward, or even if you're not and would like a little help to get you going the right way, there are many, many things I can recommend. Come to an improvement class. There are teachers I can recommend dotted around the world. Contact me, and I will see what I can do to put you in touch.*

Remember: it is what you do (or stop doing) from here on that matters. And, if you succeed in working to Alexander's principles you can expect your general standard to continually improve. In fact, if it does not, according to F M Alexander, we have evidence that points to the wrongness of the principle(s) upon which our practice is founded.[2] For F M Alexander, the test of principle is to see what happens when you work to the principle. If your general standard improves, then that is evidence in its favour. If it declines, then that is evidence against. The principles and accompanying procedures you adopt should support you in gaining a complete control of your potentialities. The principles I have articulated here have done so for me and my students. It is up to you to see what happens if you put them to work. To do so, you need an aspiration. And of course, you must be willing to change.

Finally, to teach well, you have to give something of yourself. To live well, you have to give up something of yourself. In 1955, when he died, Alexander left a legacy; it was there in the testimony of those that knew him, and also in the books he wrote, books we can read and study today. And in this particular book, more than anything, I have tried to share some of that legacy

---

*   My contact details can be found at the end of this book.

with you, in the hope that you can use it to bring about improvement in your life.

I look forward to our meeting again.

Notes

1. In Notes of Instruction in *The Alexander Technique - The Essential Writings of F M Alexander,* selected by Ed Maisel.
2. pg. xxxiii, *The Universal Constant in Living.*
3. pg. 81, *Freedom to Change.*

Additional Information

Contact information

UK and Continental Europe

If you would like to make contact with a teacher trained in the Interactive Teaching Method, or if you are interested in training to become a teacher, write to:

John Gil
ITM
PO Box 181
Bristol
BS99 7BH
enquiries@itm.demon.co.uk

The ITM Association offers Winter and Summer workshops in Germany and the UK.

North America

If you would like to make contact with a teacher trained in the Interactive Teaching Method, you may write to:

Emma Jarrett
1001 West Fraser Road
Quesnel
BC
CANADA
V2J 6P3

Contacting Anthony Taylor

Gil Books
22 Long Lodge Drive
Walton-on-Thames
Surrey, KT12 3BY
UK

Gil Books
Box No. 269
793A Foothill Boulevard
San Luis Obispo
CA, 93405 USA

info@improveyourlife.net

Selected Bibliography

Books by F M Alexander

Man's Supreme Inheritance (Mouritz, London)
Constructive Conscious Control of the Individual (Stat Books)
The Use of the Self (Gollancz)
The Universal Constant in Living (Mouritz)
Articles and Lectures (Mouritz)
The Alexander Technique - The Essential Writings of F M Alexander (edited by Ed Maisel). See Also *Aphorisms*. (Mouritz)

Books on the Interative Teaching Method

What You Think Is What You Get - Dr. Donald Weed (Gil Books)
Four Days in Bristol - Dr. Donald Weed (Gil Books)
Escape from the Monkey Hatch - Dr. Donald Weed (Gil Books)

Books on the Alexander Technique

Freedom to Change - Frank Pierce Jones (Mouritz)
Explaining the Alexander Technique - Walter Carrington (Sheildrake Press)
F M Alexander — The Man and His Work - Lulie Westfeld (Mouritz)
The Philosopher's Stone - Diaries of Lessons with F M Alexander - edited by Jean M O Fischer (Mouritz)

Other

The 7 Habits of Highly Effective People - Steven Covey (Simon & Schuster)
How to be Rich - John Paul Getty (Jove Books, New York)
The Artists Way - Julia Cameron (Pan Books)
If You Want to be Rich and Happy... - Robert Kiyosaki (Aslan)
Psycho-cybernetics - Maxwell Maltz (Pocket Books)
Feeling Good - David Burns (various)
Feel the Fear and Do it Anyway - Dr Susan Jeffers (Rider)
How to Win Friends and Influence People - Dale Carnegie (Pocket Books)
Tao Te King by Lao Tsu - rendered by Timothy Freke (Piatkus)
Help Yourself - Dave Pelzer (Thorsons)
Man's Search for Meaning - Victor Frankl (various)
I know why the caged bird sings - Maya Angelou (Virago)
An Actor Prepares - Constantin Stanislavski (Methuen)